WONDERFUL WORLD!

Christian Assemblies for Primary Schools

Michael Forster

To Glen

Most of the songs in this book can be found in *Come and Praise*,
published by BBC Books, 1990, and *Wake Up, World!*,
published by Kevin Mayhew Ltd, 1993.

First published in 1995 by
KEVIN MAYHEW LTD
Rattlesden
Bury St Edmunds
Suffolk IP30 0SZ

ISBN 0 86209 587 5
Catalogue No 1500014

© 1995 Kevin Mayhew Limited

Editor Alison Sommazzi
Cover design by Jennifer Carter
Typesetting and Page Creation by Vicky Brown
Printed in Great Britain

Foreword

These assemblies are intended for use in schools, but people who work with children in churches may also find them of value. Each assembly is based upon a particular bible story, which has been rewritten to provide added interest for children while retaining the essential point of the original. The story may be read as a narrative, or there is an alternative version with simple speaking parts for children, and this may be photocopied as necessary. The two versions may not be identical. For example, several characters have sometimes been combined for simplicity in the drama. In other cases, different slants on the story can be drawn out according to which version is used.

Suggestions are offered for ways of involving the class in the preparation work, linking the story with present day experiences and encouraging further reflection both before and during the assembly. The prayers which follow the stories also pick up some of the traditional forms of prayer: thanksgiving, confession and intercession. Finally, a number of songs are recommended for each assembly, with some newly-written ones included at the end of the book. Some will need to be learnt while others go to already known tunes, such as nursery rhymes, and yet others are well established favourites. Thanks to the skill of Christopher Tambling, the new tunes will certainly repay the effort involved.

The task of preparing this book has been very enjoyable; I hope it may be fun to use.

MICHAEL FORSTER

Acknowledgements

Thanks are due to a number of people:

Christopher Tambling who has written characteristically
singable tunes for the new songs

Jo Donlevy for her suggestions about general style
and content of the book

Phil and Jill Watts for their helpful comments
on the original draft

Hannah Mayhew and Claire Donlevy, whose enthusiasm
for *A Story, a Hug and a Prayer* encouraged me
in producing this adaptation.

Contents

A Boatful of Trouble

Based on Genesis 6:9-8:22

BEFORE THE DAY

Ask the children about their pets and in particular about how they look after them. Perhaps some children would like to draw pictures, or bring into school some photographs, for a small display board. Maybe one or two would be willing to speak just a few sentences on the subject.

• Think about the actions for all the children to join in during the story.

ON THE DAY

Introduction

Today, we're going to think about how we care for animals, and we're going to hear a story from the Bible about someone God asked to look after an awful lot of them. First, we'll say our 'Thank you' prayer.

'Thank you' Prayer

Thank you, God, for all you give us,
thank you for the earth and sea;
thank you, God, for special people,
thank you, God, for making me.

God's Story

A very long time ago, there was a man called Noah. He lived with his wife, whom everyone called Mrs. Noah (because they were terribly polite in those days) and his three sons. His sons were called Shem, Ham and Japheth, and each of them was married.

Noah was a good man; he and his family tried to live the way God wanted. They loved each other, looked after the land, cared for their animals and tried to make life as good for everyone as they could.

One day, God spoke to Noah. 'The trouble is,' he said, 'that not everyone's as caring as you are. People cheat and steal; they're cruel to each other and to the animals; they want the earth to give them lots of food, but they don't want to look after it. If they go on this way, there'll be no earth left. I want you to build a boat.'

Now if Noah hadn't known better, he'd have thought God was talking nonsense. 'A boat,' he said, 'here? Now what would I do with a boat, when there's nowhere to sail it?'

'Give me time,' said God, 'and there will be! There's going to be a flood – and you'll need the boat to live in. And you'd better make it good and big, because you're taking a lot of animals with you.'

'How many?' asked Noah.

'Two,' God answered. But before Noah could say that they wouldn't need a big boat for just two animals, God went on, '. . . of every kind of creature on earth.'

Now that *did* sound like a lot, but it was obviously no good arguing, so Noah got on with building the boat.

All the family helped. No-one had much time to rest because it was such a big boat and there wasn't much time to build it.

What do you think they did?

• They *hammered*
• They *sawed*
• They *planed*

Of course, the neighbours loved it. They really thought Noah had gone mad! 'Oh!' they shouted, 'look at Admiral Noah!' They stopped laughing, though, when the animals started to arrive. After all, zoos are very nice in their place, but whose mum or dad wants to live next door to one?

How many animals can you think of?

Well, they were all there – two of each. What a job it must have been keeping the foxes away from the chickens and stopping the mice from annoying the elephants! But eventually, they were all on board and Noah closed the hatches just as it started to rain.

Rain? You've never seen rain like it – day after day for well over a month until there was no land to be seen. But it was no pleasure cruise – Noah and his family had lots of work to do! Can you imagine looking after all those animals? And they had to make sure they were fed on time, especially the lions, or dreadful things might have happened!

No matter how hard Noah tried, the animals just wouldn't learn to get along together. The monkeys kept stealing Noah's bananas (and Noah liked bananas very much), the hyenas kept everyone awake at night, telling jokes and laughing loudly; the giraffes, of course, could see more than anyone else, and they gossiped about all the other animals; the elephants wouldn't stay in the middle of the boat, and kept making it lop-sided; and Noah threatened to swat the flies when they annoyed him. Don't you think he should have done?

Everyone was very glad when the water went down and they could all get off the ark. Then Noah said, 'Well, what do we do now?'

'What do you think?' God answered. 'You've got the chance to start again. You can make the world a much better place than it was before. And before you ask, you needn't worry because I'm never going to do this again. To show you I mean it, I'm giving you a rainbow.'

A beautiful rainbow appeared in the sky. And now, all this time later, when the rainbow appears in the sky it reminds us that God loves us and wants us to be happy.

Our Story

Display the board of pictures, and/or get the children to speak as arranged. Emphasise the importance of caring for animals as a way of showing our love for God.

Prayers

We're Glad

Heavenly Father,
you made the world,
full of colours –
plants,
animals,
and us.
We're glad about that.
Thank you for our wonderful world.

We're Sad

Sometimes we don't care for the world.
Sometimes we make it dirty,
sometimes we're cruel,
sometimes we just don't notice.
We're sorry.
Help us to care for it better.

Let's Pray for People

Thank you, loving God,
for people who care:
those who care for animals,
those who grow flowers and food,
those who teach us
and help us to understand.
Help them to do a good job,
let them know we're grateful.
And help us to care more.

Songs

There's a rainbow in the sky and it's O.K!
All of the creatures God had made
Keep on travelling on!

– from *Wake up, World!*

Morning has broken
Think of a world without any flowers
He's got the whole world in his hands
One more step along the world I go

– from *Come and Praise*

Sing a song of weather

– see *Appendix*

A Boatful of Trouble

God's Story

Narrator	A very long time ago, there was a man called Noah. He lived with his wife and three sons. They were all good people, and loved each other very much but the other people around them weren't very nice at all. One day, God spoke to Noah.
God	Noah, I want you build me a boat.
Noah	What, here? Whatever would I do with a boat when there's nowhere to sail it?
God	Just give me time, and there will be. I'm going to send a flood.
Noah	Now, why would you do a thing like that?
God	The world's in a mess, Noah, and I'm going to get rid of all the people and start again. Not you, of course. If everyone lived the way you do, there'd be no problem.
Noah	So you want me to build a boat for my family, is that it?
God	Er, no . . . not exactly. I want you to take some animals along.
Noah	How many?
God	Two . . .
Noah	Oh, that's alright – we can cope with two.
God	. . . of every kind that exists.
Noah	What? That'll be thousands.
God	Then you'd better make the boat good and big. And perhaps you should stop arguing and start building.

Narrator   So Noah and all his family got down to building the boat. What do you think they did?

- They *hammered*
- They *sawed*
- They *planed*

When they finished the boat, it was enormous. They got all the animals into it and shut the door just as the rain started. But Mrs. Noah wasn't happy.

Mrs. Noah   You didn't tell me when I married you that I was going to be cooped up on a boat with lots of animals.

Noah   I suppose you'd rather be out there, would you, in all that water?

Mrs. Noah   No, not really – but did you have to bring two of everything? I'm going to swat those flies before this is over, I can tell you.

Narrator   It was very hard – and the animals wouldn't behave themselves. The monkeys stole Noah's bananas; the hyenas kept everyone awake at night by laughing at silly jokes, and the elephants kept moving about and making the boat lop-sided. Everyone was very glad when the floods had gone and they could all get out of the boat again.

Noah   Well, I'm glad that's over!

Mrs. Noah   How d'you know it's over? God might decide to do it again, for all we know.

God   No I won't. I'm never going to do this again. And to show you I mean it, I'm giving you a rainbow.

Narrator   A beautiful rainbow appeared in the sky. And now, all this time later, when we see the rainbow it reminds us that God loves us and wants us to be happy.

Not a Lot of Brotherly Love

Based on Genesis 37:1-28

BEFORE THE DAY

What different kinds of clothes do the children wear, and why? Do they play in the garden in their best clothes? Why not? Could they make some simple 'mannequins' and dress them in different clothes, for working, for school etc? Perhaps you could get some local factories to contribute some more specialised clothing: safety helmets, gloves and so on.

• Think about the actions for all the children to join in during the story.

ON THE DAY

Introduction

Do you know the story of Joseph's special coat? We'll hear it in a minute, but first we'll say our 'Thank you' prayer.

'Thank you' Prayer

Thank you, God, for all you give us,
thank you for the earth and sea;
thank you, God, for special people,
thank you, God, for making me.

God's Story

Joseph had eleven brothers. Can you imagine that! I bet they had trouble remembering each other's names! Anyway, I'm not going to tell you all of them, or you'll be as confused as they probably were! Now I'd like to tell you what a wonderful boy Joseph was, and how much his brothers loved him. I'd like to. But I can't. The truth is that he was not really a very nice person at all, when he was young – although he improved as he got older. As a boy, he was always telling tales about his brothers – and his father believed him. Now

his father was Jacob, and he'd been no angel when he was Joseph's age. So he should have known better than to believe what Joseph was saying. Anyway, Joseph's brothers gradually got more and more fed up with the trouble Joseph caused. Then, one day, they decided they'd had enough.

'He got me into trouble again today,' said Reuben, 'saying I'd neglected the sheep; and I hadn't.'

'Well,' said Levi, who was older than Joseph but younger than Reuben, 'it wouldn't be so bad if he did any work himself, but he doesn't. And Dad's bought him a new coat. It's got *long sleeves!* He can't work in that, can he?' That was true, of course. It's not easy to work in posh clothes, is it?

- He couldn't *milk the cows*
- He couldn't *clean the windows*
- He couldn't *paint the fences*

'That's nothing,' said Reuben. 'What about all these dreams he's been telling us about – dreaming that he's the greatest, and we're all going to bow and scrape to him? I'm the eldest, and I'll tell you this: I bow and scrape to nobody!'

They decided they'd have to teach Joseph a lesson. Then, one day, when they had taken the sheep a long way away looking for some grass, they jumped on Joseph and were going to kill him.

Reuben was very worried. 'Joseph might be a stuck-up little so-and-so,' he thought, 'but he's still our brother.' So he said to the others, 'Don't kill him – just put him into one of these dried-up wells, and scare him.' He thought he could go back later and rescue Joseph.

So that's what they did. Can you imagine how Joseph felt, being left in a deep hole in the ground? He wasn't tough and brave, like his brothers, because he'd been spoilt all his life. So he was really frightened, and angry. 'You come and get me out of here!' he kept shouting out, and, 'You just wait until I tell Dad what you've done!'

'I've had enough of this!' said one of the brothers. 'The very next camel that comes along, he's on it. I don't care where it's going.'

Very soon, they saw some Egyptian traders coming across the desert on camels. They ran and got Joseph out of the hole and took him to meet them. 'Look,' they said, 'we've got something for you – a slave. Thirty pounds and he's yours.'

The trader said, 'You must be joking – he doesn't look as if he could survive a good day's work. Thirty pounds indeed! I'll take him off your hands for ten!'

'Twenty-five,' said Dan.

'No way,' said the trader. 'Twenty pounds, take it or leave it. I can't hang around here all day.'

So Joseph was sold for twenty pounds to an Egyptian trader, and soon disappeared over the horizon. The problem then was, what were his brothers going to tell their father?

'I know,' said Dan, 'let's say a wolf got him.'

And do you know – that is just what they did. Jacob was terribly upset, because he thought he would never see his favourite son again.

But of course, he was wrong.

Joseph, as we know, was still alive, although very frightened. What no-one knew at that time was that he was going to have great adventures in Egypt.

But we'll have to hear about that another time.

Our Story

Ask the children to look at the display and work out what the different kinds of clothes are for. Get the children thinking and talking about the different kinds of work that happen in their house and what their part is in it.

Prayers

We're Glad

Dear God,
thank you for our families and friends;
thank you for the things we do together.
Thank you for the fun we have,
for the games we play,
(*and especially for . . .*)

We're Sad

Loving God,
some people don't like us,
and sometimes we don't like them.
We get unhappy,
cross,
selfish,
but you still love us.
Thank you for loving us,
and please help us to love one another.

Let's Pray for People

Let's pray for people we don't see very often.
Thank you, God,
for our friends and relatives
who live far away.
Keep them safe,
and let them know
that we love them.

Songs

We can plough and dig the land
Keep on travelling on!
God is making a wonderful world

– from *Wake up, World!*

God knows me
When I needed a neighbour
Kum ba yah

– from *Come and Praise*

Not a Lot of Brotherly Love

God's Story

Narrator Joseph had eleven brothers. Can you imagine that!
I bet they had trouble remembering each other's names!
Anyway, I'm not going to tell you all of them, or you'll
be as confused as they probably were!

Now I'd like to tell you what a wonderful boy Joseph
was, and how his brothers loved him. I'd like to. But I
can't. The truth is that he was not a very nice person
at all, when he was young – although he improved as
he got older. As a boy, he was always telling tales about
his brothers – and his father believed him. Now his
father was Jacob, and he'd been no angel when he was
Joseph's age. So he should have known better than to
believe what Joseph was saying.

Anyway, one day, Reuben told Levi he'd had enough.

Reuben That brother of ours got me into trouble again today,
saying I'd neglected the sheep; and I hadn't.

Levi It wouldn't be so bad if he did any work himself,
but he doesn't. And now Dad's bought him a new coat.
It's got *long* sleeves! He can't work in that, can he?

Narrator That's true. Joseph couldn't do hard work wearing
fancy clothes, could he?

- He couldn't *milk the cows*
- He couldn't *clean the windows*
- He couldn't *paint the fences*

No wonder the brothers were angry. They were
going to have to do Joseph's share of the work!

Reuben That's nothing! What about all these dreams he's been
telling us about – dreaming that he's the greatest,
and we're all going to bow and scrape to him? I'm the
eldest, and I'll tell you this: I bow and scrape to nobody!

Narrator	The brothers got together and decided to teach Joseph a lesson. Then, one day, when they had taken the sheep a long way away looking for some grass, they jumped on Joseph and were going to kill him. Reuben was very worried.
Reuben	Joseph might be a stuck-up little so-and-so, but he's still our brother. Don't kill him – just put him into one of these dried-up wells, and scare him.
Narrator	Can you imagine how Joseph felt, being left in a deep hole in the ground? He wasn't tough and brave, like his brothers, because he'd been spoilt all his life. So he was really frightened and angry and he wouldn't stop shouting.
Joseph	You come and get me out of here! You just wait until I tell Dad what you've done!
Levi	I've had enough of this! The very next camel that comes along, he's on it. I don't care where it's going.
Narrator	Very soon, they saw some Egyptian traders coming across the desert on camels. They ran and got Joseph out of the hole, and took him to meet them. They wanted thirty pounds for him but the traders beat them down to twenty. They handed Joseph over to the traders and watched as their camels disappeared over the horizon. Then they had another problem.
Reuben	What are we going to tell Dad?
Levi	I know. Let's say a wolf got him.
Narrator	And do you know – that is just what they did. Jacob was terribly upset, because he thought he would never see his favourite son again. But of course, he was wrong. Joseph, as we know, was still alive, although very frightened. What no-one knew at that time was that he was going to have great adventures in Egypt. But we'll have to hear about that another time.

Joseph's Adventures

Based on Genesis 40-41

BEFORE THE DAY

Have the children visited interesting places (perhaps on a school trip)? Could they draw pictures about them? Perhaps they have some snapshots or souvenirs they could bring to display in the assembly.

• Think about the actions for all the children to join in during the story.

ON THE DAY

Introduction

We're going to hear about some of Joseph's adventures in Egypt, but first we'll say our 'Thank you' prayer.

'Thank you' Prayer

Thank you, God, for all you give us,
thank you for the earth and sea;
thank you, God, for special people,
thank you, God, for making me.

God's Story

This is a story about Joseph, who was taken to Egypt as a slave. He was soon in trouble again and finished up in prison. It wasn't his fault – someone who didn't like him very much told lies about him. That's what he used to do about his brothers, and he learnt that it wasn't funny when it happened to him! But while he was in prison his adventures started.

Anthony, the palace barman, was there as well. 'What have you done?' asked Joseph.

'Mind your own business!' replied Anthony, which wasn't very friendly. Joseph kept quiet after that, as he had learnt not to upset people if he could help it. But next morning, Anthony was very quiet and thoughtful. He didn't say a word! He sat in a corner of the cell and . . .

• He *scratched* his head
• He *stroked* his chin
• He *shook* his head from side to side

'What's the matter?' asked Joseph, expecting to get told to mind his own business again. But Anthony was much nicer.

'I've had a funny dream,' he said. 'I was standing beside this grapevine with three branches. While I was there, grapes grew on the branches.'

'What did you do?' asked Joseph.

'What I'm here to do,' replied Anthony. 'I squeezed the grapes, and made some wine for the king.'

'Well, that's easy to understand,' said Joseph, 'each branch is like one day. So you'll be out of here and back in your job in three days.'

Anthony couldn't believe it when that came true! Of course, he could have told the king and perhaps got Joseph released, but he forgot. He was not at all grateful.

Two years later, the king had strange dreams which no-one in the palace could explain. Then the barman remembered. He went to the king and said, 'I'm terribly sorry - I forgot to tell you – I had a dream when I was in prison.'

'Don't come bothering me with your dreams!' the king snapped. 'I'm too worried about my own.'

'That's just it, Your Majesty,' answered Anthony. 'There was a prisoner called Joseph – foreign chap – and he told me what the dream meant.' So Joseph was sent for.

'It's like this,' said the king. 'I dreamt that I was standing by the river when seven fat cows came up from the water and stood on the bank.'

Anthony interrupted, 'Er . . . what kind of cows were they, Your Majesty – were they brown or black?'

'Don't interrupt!' said the king. 'Or you'll find yourself back in prison.'

'Well!' thought Anthony. 'I only asked!'

'As I was saying,' the king went on, 'there were these seven fat cows. Then up came seven thin cows, and ate all the fat ones! Now what could that mean?'

'That's easy!' said Joseph. 'The cows are like years. There will be seven good years – plenty of food, people will have jobs, and no-one will go hungry. But then there'll be seven bad years, without any rain. The crops won't grow, there'll be no water, people will lose their jobs, and a lot of people will go hungry. And it will be just as if the seven good years had never happened.'

'That's terrible!' said the king. 'What can we do?'

'You need some help, Your Majesty,' said Joseph. 'Put someone who's really wise and clever in charge of the country. You've got to save as much as you can in the good years, to see you through the bad.'

'Well,' said the king, 'I can't think of anyone wiser or cleverer than you. So it looks as though you've got the job.'

That was how Joseph became a very important person in Egypt. For the first seven years, he made sure that as much food as possible was saved. Then the bad years came. No food was growing anywhere, not in Egypt and not in the countries round about, either. But no-one starved in Egypt, because Joseph had done his job so well.

Our Story

Draw attention to the 'travel' display. Joseph was in a foreign country. He met some very interesting people and had wonderful adventures. And they found out that 'foreign chaps' bring their own special gifts with them, as well.

Prayers

We're Glad

Wonderful God,
you give us so much.
Thank you for the things we see and hear,
thank you for the people we meet.
(*Especially . . .*)

We're Sad

Sometimes, we're so happy
that we don't notice other people
who aren't.
Sometimes, we're so full of ourselves
that we forget to say 'Thank you'.
We're sorry.
Help us to notice other people,
and to love them.

Let's Pray for People

Let's say 'thank you' to God
for people who are nice to us.
Loving God,
we remember our friends
and people who help us.
Thank you for them.
Thank you for all the things we like about them:
let them know how we appreciate them,
and help us to show it more ourselves.

Songs

Pick up your feet and go!
We can plough and dig the land
Keep on travelling on!

– from *Wake up, World!*

Somebody greater
God knows me
When I needed a neighbour

– from *Come and Praise*

Joseph's Adventures

God's Story

Narrator   This is a story about Joseph, who was taken to Egypt as a slave. He was soon in trouble again, and finished up in prison. Someone told lies about him. That's what he used to do about his brothers, and he learnt that it wasn't funny, when it happened to him! But then his adventures started. Anthony, the palace barman, was there as well. So Joseph tried to make polite conversation.

Joseph   What have you done to get put in here?

Anthony   Mind your own business!

Narrator   Joseph, kept quiet after that, as he had learnt not to upset people if he could help it. But next morning, Anthony was very thoughtful. He just sat in the corner of his cell, and . . .

- He *scratched* his head
- He *stroked* his chin
- He *shook* his head from side to side

Joseph couldn't contain his curiosity any longer.

Joseph   What's the matter? I hope you don't mind me asking!

Anthony   No – sorry about yesterday – I've had a funny dream. I was standing beside this grapevine with three branches. While I was there, grapes grew on the branches.

Joseph   What did you do?

Anthony   What I'm here to do – I squeezed the grapes, and made some wine for the king.

Joseph   Well, that's easy to understand. In your dream, each branch is like one day. So you'll be out of here and back in your job in three days.

Narrator   Anthony couldn't believe it when that came true! Of course, he could have told the king and perhaps got Joseph released, but he forgot. He was not at all grateful.

    Two years later, the king had strange dreams, which no-one in the palace could explain. Then the barman remembered.

Anthony	I'm terribly sorry – I forgot to tell you – I had a dream, when I was in prison.
King	Don't come bothering me with your dreams! I'm too worried about my own.
Anthony	That's just it, Your Majesty. There was a prisoner called Joseph – foreign chap – and he told me what the dream meant.
Narrator	So Joseph was sent for.
King	It's like this: I dreamt that I was standing by the river, when seven fat cows came up from the water, and stood on the bank.
Anthony	Er . . . what kind of cows were they, Your Majesty – were they brown or black?
King	Don't interrupt, or you'll find yourself back in prison.
Anthony	Well! I only asked!
King	As I was saying, there were these seven fat cows. Then up came seven thin cows, and ate all the fat ones! Now what could that mean?
Joseph	That's easy! The cows are like years. There will be seven good years – plenty of food, and no-one will go hungry. But then there'll be seven bad years, without any rain, and in the end it will be just as if the seven good years had never happened.
King	That's terrible! What can we do?
Joseph	You need some help, Your Majesty. Put someone who's really wise and clever in charge of the country. You've got to save as much as you can in the good years, to see you through the bad.
King	Well I can't think of anyone wiser or cleverer than you. So it looks as though you've got the job.
Narrator	That was how Joseph became a very important person in Egypt. For the first seven years, he made sure that as much food as possible was saved. Then the bad years came. No food was growing anywhere, not in Egypt and not in the countries round about, either. But no-one starved in Egypt, because Joseph had done his job so well.

Baby in the Bulrushes

Based on Exodus 2:1-10

BEFORE THE DAY

Ask the children whether they have ever had a nice surprise. Perhaps they expected to be told off, and were praised instead; maybe they thought they had lost something, and it turned out to be safe; or possibly they were worried about someone who was ill, who unexpectedly got better.

• Think about the actions for all the children to join in during the story.

ON THE DAY

Introduction

We all love nice surprises. Sometimes, just when we expect things to go wrong, something happens to put them right. It doesn't always work out of course, but it's wonderful when it does. First, we'll say our 'Thank you' prayer.

'Thank you' Prayer

Thank you, God, for all you give us,
thank you for the earth and sea;
thank you, God, for special people,
thank you, God, for making me.

God's Story

A very long time ago, in a place called Egypt, lived a really bad king. He made all the foreign people in his country into slaves. They had to work all day long in the hot sun, making bricks, moving heavy stones about and doing all the jobs that the king didn't want his own people to have to do.

Then the king got frightened. He didn't like the children in slave families especially the little boys. 'Little boys grow up into men,' he thought, 'and men fight. What if one day they get fed up with being slaves, and attack me?' So he did a horrible thing. He tried to kill all the boy babies.

There was a little girl called Miriam in one of the slave families. She was really pleased because she had a new baby brother. But her parents were very worried, because they knew what the king would do if he found out. What do you think they did? They put the little baby boy into a special waterproof basket, and hid it in the bulrushes with Miriam hiding nearby and watching.

Imagine how horrified she was when a princess from the king's palace came along to swim in the river! 'Oh dear!' thought Miriam, 'I hope they don't find the baby!'

But of course the princess soon noticed the basket in the reeds. She opened it, and cried out, 'Oh what a beautiful baby! But he's crying. He must be frightened, poor little thing!'

So what do you think the princess did?

• She *lifted* him up
• She *hugged* him
• She *rocked* him

'What should I do now?' thought Miriam. 'I know – I'll pretend to be just passing by, and see if I can help.'

So she strolled along the river bank, humming a little tune to herself, until she accidentally-on-purpose bumped into the princess. 'Ooh! What a lovely baby!' she said, pretending never to have seen him before.

'Yes,' said the princess, 'I think he's a foreign baby. He's so beautiful and I would love to keep him. So, since no-one knows whose he is, I'll take him back to the palace.'

Then Miriam had a wonderful idea. 'Shall I get you a nurse for him?' she asked, 'After all, you wouldn't want to do everything yourself, Your Highness!'

'What a good idea!' said the princess. 'Go and find a woman from among the foreign slave people, who can nurse him for me.'

Well, Miriam raced home as fast as she could, and went bursting into her home, gasping for breath. 'Really, Miriam!' said her father. 'How many times must I tell you to be more ladylike? Charging around like that, anyone would think something exciting was happening!'

Miriam could hardly talk, she was so out of breath. All she could do was point towards the river, while gasping for air! 'What on earth's the matter?' asked Mum, 'It isn't the baby, is it?' and she began to get very agitated indeed.

By now, Miriam was getting her breath back. 'A princess . . .' she spluttered, 'by . . . river . . . found . . . baby . . . needs a nurse.'

They all hurried back to the river. There they found the princess still holding the baby. Taking a deep breath, Miriam went up to her and said, 'I've found someone who can nurse the baby for you.'

'Good!' smiled the princess, who was nowhere near as horrible as her father; in fact she was rather nice, 'You realise you'll have to live at the palace?'

'Of course,' said Mum. The princess handed over the baby. 'He's a lovely little thing,' she said. 'I wish I knew who his parents are.'

Of course, no-one told her, because that would have been too dangerous. But they all set off to the palace together. Miriam was really excited about living in a real palace, with a real live princess – nearly as excited as she was about having a baby brother.

'What are you going to call the baby?' she asked.

'I think I'll call him Moses,' answered the princess.

So the baby was taken to the palace, along with the 'nurse' who was really his mother, and the princess treated him just like one of the royal family.

Our Story

Tell the school about the stories you shared in preparation. Perhaps some of the children in other classes have something to add? Things don't always work out as well as they did for Miriam's family, but life does have its nice surprises.

Prayers

We're Glad

Amazing God!
Life can be so exciting!
We never know what might happen!
Sometimes, people are nice to us,
when we don't expect it.
Lovely things happen,
which we haven't planned.
Thank you for a wonderful world,
full of surprises.

We're Sad

We're sorry, God,
for letting people down.
We're sorry for not being
as good as we could be.
Help us to give people nice surprises,
not nasty shocks.

Let's Pray for People

God, our friend,
we pray for happy people
(*especially . . .*)
Thank you for their happiness.
Help us to show them
that we're happy, too.
And we pray for unhappy people
(*especially . . .*)
Let them know that we care,
and that we're sad for them.

Songs

Out to the great wide world we go
God made the earth

– from *Wake up, World!*

He's got the whole world in his hands
Water of life
Kum ba yah
Morning has broken

– from *Come and Praise*

Baby in the Bulrushes

God's Story

Narrator   A very long time ago, in a place called Egypt, lived a really bad king. In his country were some people of another race, and he hated them. He made them work as slaves. Then he did something very evil, and decided to kill all their boy babies. So when a little girl called Miriam found she had a new baby brother she was very pleased, but also very frightened.

Miriam   Mum, I've got an idea. Why don't we hide the baby in a basket? If we cover it in tar, it will float, and then we can hide it in the rushes at the side of the river.

Narrator   So that's what they did. They put the little baby boy into the basket, and hid it in the bulrushes. Miriam decided to hide nearby and keep an eye on it, just in case. Imagine how horrified she was when a princess from the king's palace came along to swim in the river! The princess went into the water and began to swim, and then noticed the basket in the reeds. She opened it and saw the baby.

Princess   Oh what a beautiful baby! But he's crying. He must be frightened, poor little thing!

Narrator   So, what do you think the princess did?

- She *lifted* him up
- She *hugged* him
- She *rocked* him

Miriam was very worried. So she strolled along the river bank, humming a little tune to herself, until she accidentally-on-purpose bumped into the princess.

Miriam   Ooh! What a lovely baby! Is he yours?

Princess   No, I think he's a foreign baby. He's so beautiful, and I would love to keep him. So, since no-one knows whose he is, I'll take him back to the palace.

Miriam   Er, would you like me to try and find a nurse for him? After all, you wouldn't want to do *everything* yourself, Your Highness!

Princess   What a good idea. Go and find a woman from among the foreign slave people who can nurse him for me.

Narrator   Well, Miriam raced home as fast as she could and went bursting into her home, gasping for breath.

Mum   What on earth's the matter? It isn't the baby, is it?

Miriam   *(Breathlessly)* It's a princess . . . by the river . . . found the baby . . . wants a nurse!

Narrator   So Miriam and Mum hurried back to the river, and found the princess still there, holding the baby.

Miriam   Er . . . Your Highness, I've found a woman who can act as a nurse for you.

Princess   That's fine. *(Turns to Mum)* You don't mind coming to live at the palace?

Mum   Not at all. Um . . . can I ask what you're going to call him?

Princess   I think I'll call him Moses.

Narrator   So the baby was taken to the palace, along with the 'nurse' who was really his mother, and the princess treated him just like one of the royal family.

Escaping Through the Sea

Based on Exodus 14

BEFORE THE DAY

Ask the children about exciting journeys they've been on (if they have included an element of risk, so much the better). Have any of them been to a wildlife park, or on a rollercoaster ride? Did they get any souvenirs? Perhaps they'd like to bring them into school, so that you can make up a display. Or they could draw pictures and stick them on a board. Would some of them like to describe their journeys? If they were a little nervous about going, for example, in a ship or aeroplane (or perhaps only their families were!) then that would be interesting to know as well.

• Think about the actions for all the children to join in during the story.

ON THE DAY
Introduction

This morning, we're going to hear about some journeys, but first we'll say our 'Thank you' prayer.

'Thank you' Prayer

Thank you, God, for all you give us,
thank you for the earth and sea;
thank you, God, for special people,
thank you, God, for making me.

God's Story

Moses grew up in the royal palace in Egypt, but he had always felt a little different. He never liked the way the wicked king hurt the foreign slaves, and one day, after a lot of arguments with the king, he led all the slaves out into the desert to find a new home.

'Where are we going?' they asked.
'I'm not really sure,' said Moses, 'but God has told me it's a wonderful place. There's plenty of food there, and lots of milk and honey. And most of all, you'll be free!'

Among the people was a trouble-maker called Simon. He'd never really liked Moses, and he certainly didn't like the desert. He thought he would stir up a bit of bother.

'Big deal!' he said. 'I don't see any sign of that here – there's nothing but sand, heat and flies! What have you brought us out here for? We might have been slaves in Egypt, but at least we got fed!'

Then everyone else started complaining, too. They'd already forgotten how dreadful life had been in Egypt!

Meanwhile, back in Egypt, the wicked king was getting complaints from *his* people, as well. They didn't like having to weed their own gardens and wash their own chariots. So, for the sake of a quiet life, the king sent the army to recapture the slaves.

The Israelite people were camped at the shore of the Reed Sea, which was really a very big lake. (Most people think it was the Red Sea, but you all know better now, don't you?)

'Well!' said Simon, 'Another fine mess you've got us into! We can't get across, and it's an awfully long way round – and the army's catching up with us.'

Moses wasn't too worried. He knew God would help him.

How do you think they might have got across?

- They might have *swum*
  (but it was much too far)
- They might have *rowed*
  (but they hadn't any boats)
- They might have *flown*
  (but no-one had invented aeroplanes)
- They might have *walked*
  (but it was too deep)

Then God said a strange thing. 'Don't come crying to me,' he said, 'but tell the people to move forward,' which was a funny thing to say because that meant walking right into the sea. Well, they dithered about, trying to decide who should go first. Eventually, Moses reached out his hand over the sea, and the most amazing thing happened. The sea separated, to the left and right, and there was a pathway of dry land straight through the middle of it.

- So they didn't have to *swim*
- And they didn't have to *row*
- And they didn't have to *fly*
- They only had to *walk*

'That's it!' shouted Moses, 'Now let's go!' Simon still wasn't convinced.

'That's an awful lot of water piled up at each side,' he said, 'and how do we know it won't come down on us?'

But he either had to trust God or sit and wait to be captured by the Egyptians. So he decided to risk it. And anyway, by that time, the others were on their way. Down to the sea bed they went, with their donkeys, their carts, and everything they had. As they walked along they could see the water on either side of them, and hear the great wind blowing, keeping it apart. Well, it seemed like ages they were down on the sea bed, but eventually they started walking uphill, and knew they were near the opposite shore.

When they got there, Simon still wasn't satisfied. 'If we can do that,' he said, 'so can the Egyptians!'

'The difference is,' said Moses, 'that they haven't got God on their side.' With that, he stretched out his hand again and the wind stopped. The water came rushing back together again, splashing all over the place, with great waves leaping up as the two walls of water met. The noise was deafening! But even louder than the noise of the water was the sound of singing. The Israelite people were celebrating, because now they knew that God really was going to lead them to their promised land.

Our Story

Point out items and/or pictures on the display. Talk about the mixture of excitement and nervousness on a journey. We only go on journeys with people we trust.

Prayers

We're Glad

Let's say 'thank you' to God
for this big and exciting world.
Loving God,
thank you for showing us new things.
Whenever we start to think
that we know everything,
you show us something new!
Thank you for helping us to learn.

We're Sad

God, forgive us
for not trusting you,
and for not trusting each other.
We don't know very much
about the world,
and we make lots of mistakes.
Help us to trust you more.

Let's Pray for People

Creator God,
you made the world
for us to enjoy.
We pray for people who are unhappy.
Perhaps they think no-one cares.
Help us to show them that we do,
and help them to learn again
what a wonderful world this is.

Songs

We're all going to the Promised Land
Keep on travelling on!
Pick up your feet and go!

– from *Wake up, World!*

Morning has broken
Who put the colours in the rainbow?
One more step

– from *Come and Praise*

Escaping Through the Sea

God's Story

Narrator Our story is about Moses, the slave child who grew up in the royal palace in Egypt, He had always felt a little different. He never liked the way the wicked king hurt the foreign slaves, and one day, after a lot of arguments with the king, he led all the slaves out into the desert to find a new home. When they asked him where they were going, he seemed a bit vague about it.

Moses I'm not exactly sure where we're going, but God has told me it's a wonderful place. There's plenty of food there, plenty of cream cakes and sweets. And most of all, you'll be free!

Narrator Among the people was a trouble-maker called Simon. He'd never really liked Moses, and he certainly didn't like the desert. He thought he would stir up a bit of bother.

Simon What have you brought us out here for? There's nothing but sand, heat and flies! We might have been slaves in Egypt, but at least we got fed!

Narrator Then everyone else started complaining, too. They'd already forgotten how dreadful life had been in Egypt! Meanwhile, back in Egypt, the wicked king was getting complaints from *his* people, as well. They didn't like doing their own washing up, and they wanted their slaves back. So the king sent the army after them, and the Israelite people ended up with the evil king's army on one side of them and a great big sea on the other.

Simon Well! Here's another fine mess you've got us into! We can't get across the water, and it's an awfully long way round.

Moses Don't worry! God will get us across. He won't let us down.

Narrator   So there they were, at the edge of the sea, and somehow they had to get across. What do you think they did?

- They might have *swum* (but it was much too far)
- They might have *rowed* (but they hadn't any boats)
- They might have *flown* (but there were no aeroplanes)
- They might have *walked* (but it was too deep)

Well, it does look bad, doesn't it? But Moses knew what to do.

Moses   I said God would help. All I have to do is reach out over the water, like this, and God will do the rest.

Narrator   And he was right. God did an amazing thing! He pushed the sea back on either side and made a path right through the middle.

- So they didn't have to *swim*
- And they didn't have to *row*
- And they didn't have to *fly*
- They only had to *walk*

But Simon still wasn't convinced.

Simon   That's an awful lot of water piled up at each side, and how do we know it won't come down on us?

Moses   You don't – you've just got to trust God. But of course, you can always wait here and be captured.

Simon   All right, I'll walk – but I'm not happy.

Narrator   So they all went across. It was frightening, all right, with all that water piled up on either side. But eventually they got across, and God let the water close up again to stop the army from following. Now they were safe, and it was time to celebrate.

Moses   Yes, but not for long. We've still got a long journey ahead of us.

The Walls Came Tumbling Down

Based on Joshua 6

BEFORE THE DAY

Do the children like music? What kind? Or perhaps they just enjoy making a noise! Discuss with them the different kinds of noise. Do any of them play instruments? Would they play a short tune (or even just a few notes) in assembly? Do they have toys which make less pleasant noises? Perhaps one or two of them could be brought in for the assembly. (You might prefer to have the toys placed at the front, and not in the hands of the children!) What about unpleasant noises that are good, e.g. fire alarms?

• Think about the actions for all the children to join in during the story.

ON THE DAY

Introduction

We're going to think about noise in this assembly. Sometimes it's good, but sometimes it's bad. First, we say our 'Thank you' prayer.

'Thank you' Prayer

Thank you, God, for all you give us,
thank you for the earth and sea;
thank you, God, for special people,
thank you, God, for making me.

God's Story

Joshua wasn't happy. 'I wish,' he said, 'that Moses had never passed this job on to me! Being the leader of the Israelites is not easy!'

Joshua had taken over as leader when Moses died. Now he faced a real problem. Between his people and their new home stood a big city called Jericho. And around Jericho were some very high walls.

Meanwhile, the people in the city had seen the Israelites coming, and a soldier called Seth was giving orders. 'Hurry up and get those gates shut,' he shouted, 'or they'll be marching in here. That's better – now pile everything you can get up against them.'

Before long, the gate was completely hidden behind an enormous pile of tables, benches, boxes, rocks and all kinds of other things. Someone had even brought a baby's cradle! 'There!' said Seth, 'That should keep them out!'

What Seth didn't know was that Joshua wasn't going to attack the gates. God had better ideas. 'Don't worry about the gates,' he told Joshua, 'you're going to bring down the walls!'

Joshua could hardly believe his ears. 'Those walls must be ten feet thick!' he said.

'What's the matter,' asked God, 'haven't you ever heard of vibration? March the people round the walls every day for a week, and at the end of it you'll be able to shake the walls down by shouting.'

Well! Can you imagine the sight? Round and round they went, with soldiers in the front blowing their trumpets as loudly as they could. The enemy soldiers on top of the walls thought it was a great joke. Before long, they were selling tickets, and people were queuing up to buy them.

'Come and see the silly Israelites walking round the wall!' shouted Seth, and every day more people came to watch.

The Israelite people didn't like the job much – people shouted insults at them and dropped rubbish from the walls – but Joshua made them carry on going round. Then at last, after a week, he shouted, 'All right, let them have it!'

And what do you think they did?

• They *blew their trumpets*
• They *banged their drums*
• They *stamped their feet*
• They *shouted*

You never heard a noise like it (even just now!) The air shook with the noise, and the ground shook with the stamping of feet, and the people watching thought it was great fun – until the walls began to shake as well. Then, gradually, cracks started to appear in the walls. The cracks got bigger, and the walls began to sway, and then there was a great CRRRRRASH! The walls had fallen down. Poor old Seth was amazed, and just stood there scratching his head.

The Israelites could hardly believe what had happened. 'All we did was shout,' someone said, 'and the walls just came tumbling down!'

'Well, there you are,' smiled Joshua. 'It's amazing how much damage a bit of noise can do!'

Our Story

Demonstrate some of the 'instruments'. Some noises are nice – others aren't. But some 'bad' noises are necessary.

Prayers

We're Glad

Creator God,
thank you for music,
for singing;
thank you for making us able to talk,
and to hear.
But thank you for quietness, too,
and help us to know
when to sing and shout,
and when to be quiet.

We're Sad

Let's say 'sorry' to God
for the times we've upset people
by being too noisy.
We're sorry, God, for being thoughtless.
We don't mean to upset others,
but sometimes we're so busy enjoying ourselves
that we forget them.
Help us to remember other people.

Let's Pray for People

Loving God,
we pray for people who can't speak,
and for people who can't hear,
(*especially* . . .)
Help them to find other ways
of enjoying your world,
and having fun.
And please help us
to remember them,
and not to let them be left out.

Songs

Pick up your feet and go!
Keep on travelling on!

– from *Wake up, World!*

Morning has broken
He's got the whole world in his hands
One more step

– from *Come and Praise*

The Walls Came Tumbling Down
God's Story

Narrator Joshua had taken over as leader when Moses died. And he wasn't happy. Between his people and their new home stood a big city, called Jericho, and around Jericho were some very high walls. The people in the city had seen the Israelites coming, and a soldier called Seth was giving orders.

Seth Hurry up and get those gates shut or they'll be marching in here. That's better – now pile everything you can get up against them.

Narrator Before long, the gate was completely hidden behind an enormous pile of tables, benches, boxes, rocks and all kinds of other things. Someone had even brought a baby's cradle!

Seth There! That should keep them out! It'll take more than their little army to get through the gates now.

Narrator Now, Joshua was *really* fed up. And he thought it was time he told God so.

Joshua I wish Moses had never passed this job on to me! Being the leader of the Israelites is not easy! How are we ever going to break those gates down?

God Oh, don't worry about the gates; you're going to bring down the walls!

Joshua What?! Those walls must be ten feet thick!

God What's the matter? Haven't you ever heard of vibration? March the people round the walls every day for a week, and at the end of it you'll be able to shake the walls down by shouting.

Narrator Well! Can you imagine the sight? Round and round they went, with soldiers in the front blowing their trumpets as loudly as they could. The enemy soldiers on top of the walls thought it was a great joke. Before long, they were selling tickets, and people were queuing up to buy them.

Seth Roll up! Roll up! Come and see the silly Israelites walking round the wall!

Narrator Every day more people came to watch. The Israelite people didn't like the job much – people shouted insults at them and dropped rubbish from the walls – but Joshua made them carry on going round. Then at last, after a week, he gave the command.

Joshua All right, let them have it!

Narrator And what do you think they did?

- They *blew their trumpets*
- They *banged their drums*
- They *stamped their feet*
- They *shouted*

You never heard a noise like it (even just now!) The air shook with the noise, and the ground shook with the stamping of feet, and the people watching thought it was great fun – until the walls began to shake as well. Then, gradually, cracks started to appear in the walls. The cracks got bigger, and the walls began to sway, and then there was a great CRRRRRASH! The walls had fallen down. Poor old Seth was amazed, and just stood there scratching his head.

Seth I can't believe it! All you did was shout and the walls just came tumbling down!

Joshua Well, there you are. It's amazing how much damage a bit of noise can do!

A Love Story

Based on the Book of Ruth

BEFORE THE DAY

Have the children attended weddings? What do they remember about them? Perhaps they can draw pictures of weddings. Why not collect some wedding regalia – perhaps even dress up some models? The possibilities for involving the children are endless – right down to a mock wedding!

If a rabbi could be invited to speak at the assembly about Jewish weddings, that would be excellent.

• Think about the actions for all the children to join in during the story.

ON THE DAY

Introduction

We're going to hear a famous love story from the Bible in a few moments, but first we'll say our 'Thank you' prayer.

'Thank you' Prayer

Thank you, God, for all you give us,
thank you for the earth and sea;
thank you, God, for special people,
thank you, God, for making me.

God's Story

This is the story of Ruth. Ruth was very happy with her husband, Chilion, and together they looked after his widowed mother, Naomi. Then something dreadful happened: Chilion died. In those days, there were not many well-paid jobs for women, so without a husband life would be hard. So Naomi said, 'Ruth, you must go and find another husband – don't worry about me.'

'But what will you do?' Ruth asked, 'How will you live?'

'You mustn't worry about that,' said Naomi. 'You are young and beautiful, and on your own you will find a husband, but not if you have an old lady living with you.'

It was certainly true that Ruth could easily have married again, but she couldn't leave Naomi. 'Whatever happens,' she said, 'we'll face it together. I'm not leaving you.'

'Well,' said Naomi, 'I hear they've had a good harvest in my home town. Let's go back there.' So they set out for Naomi's home town, which was Bethlehem. (Have you heard of that before, somewhere?)

When they arrived, Naomi's family were really glad to see her, but sad that her husband had died.

Now, Naomi had a very rich relative in Bethlehem, called Boaz. And he was very kind as well (which was lucky, because not all rich people are). Ruth got a job working in his fields. She went behind the people who picked the corn, and collected up anything they dropped. Naomi told Boaz all about Ruth's loyalty. 'I kept telling her to leave me and take care of herself,' Naomi said, 'but all she would say was, "Whatever comes, we'll face it together."'

'She's obviously a very special person,' said Boaz. 'Everyone's talking about how hard she works. I must find a way of repaying her.'

So the next day, Boaz spoke to the workers. 'Drop a little extra corn,' he said, 'and let Ruth pick it up. Oh, and make sure no-one gives her any trouble.'

While Ruth was working, Boaz came and asked her, 'What are you doing for lunch?'

'Oh, don't worry about me,' said Ruth. 'I'll just sit under the cedar tree to eat my bread and fruit.'

'Well,' said Boaz, 'I'd be very pleased if you'd come and have lunch with me.'

Ruth was really pleased about that, and from then on she joined Boaz for lunch every day. They spent a lot of time together, and they soon realised that they were not 'just good friends', any more! Eventually, Boaz plucked up the courage to ask Ruth to marry him. Of course, she said, 'Yes!' because Boaz was a good, and kind man, and Ruth had come to love him very much indeed.

It was a wonderful wedding. All the other

farm workers came, along with the bride and bridegroom's friends, and of course Naomi had pride of place among them. Ruth looked absolutely beautiful, and Boaz looked pretty good, too, in his best clothes. Everyone had a wonderful time – they sang, they danced and they kept on drinking a toast!

- They *raised their glasses*
- They *shouted, 'To life!'*
- And then they *drank* every drop!

After it was all over, Ruth and Boaz went and settled down to begin their life together in his house. Before long, they had some good news for everyone. Ruth was going to have a baby. Well, of course, there was more singing, more dancing, more shouts of 'To life!' Everyone was happy, and no-one more so than Ruth and Boaz. There again, perhaps there was one other person who was at least as happy as they were. Can you guess who that was?

Of course, it was Naomi. She was so happy she could hardly stand still – because she was going to be a grandma!

Our Story

Use the display to talk about how we celebrate marriage. The romance is lovely, but as well as that, Ruth and Boaz had friendship.

If a rabbi is present, ask him or her to speak here about the kinds of things involved in a Jewish wedding and what they signify.

Prayers

We're Glad

God, our friend,
thank you for the friends you give us.
Sometimes we need them very much,
and it's good to know
they won't let us down.
Thank you for being our best friend,
the one we know we can trust,
even more than the others.

We're Sad

Loving God, we're sorry
for letting people down,
and for letting you down.
Make us more loving,
more careful,
more like you.

Let's Pray for People

Caring God,
we trust you,
and we trust each other.
We know there are people who are frightened,
who think they have no friends,
who dare not trust anybody
because they've been let down.
Help them to find friends,
and help them to trust you.

Songs

I'm black, I'm white, I'm short, I'm tall
God made the earth
Keep on travelling on!

– from *Wake up, World!*

Morning has broken
When I needed a neighbour
Black and white

– from *Come and Praise*

Thank you, O God, for all our friends

– see *Appendix*

A Love Story

God's Story

Narrator   This is the story of Ruth. Ruth was very happy with her husband, Chilion, and together they looked after his widowed mother, Naomi. Then something dreadful happened: Chilion died. In those days, there were not many well-paid jobs for women, so without a husband life would be hard. Naomi was concerned about Ruth.

Naomi   Ruth, you must go and find another husband – don't worry about me.

Ruth   But what will you do? How will you live?

Naomi   You mustn't worry about that; you are young and beautiful, and on your own you will find a husband, but not if you have an old lady living with you.

Ruth   Whatever happens, we'll face it together. I'm not leaving you.

Naomi   Well, I hear they've had a good harvest in my home town. Let's go back there.

Narrator   So they set out for Naomi's home town, which was Bethlehem. (Have you heard of that before, somewhere?) When they arrived, Naomi's family were really glad to see her but sad that her husband had died.

   Now, Naomi had a very rich relative in Bethlehem, called Boaz. And he was very kind, as well (which was lucky, because not all rich people are). Ruth got a job working in his fields. She went behind the people who picked the corn, and collected up anything they dropped. Naomi told Boaz all about Ruth's loyalty.

Naomi   I kept telling her to leave me and take care of herself, but all she would say was, 'Whatever comes, we'll face it together.'

Boaz   She's obviously a very special person; everyone's talking about how hard she works. I must find a way of repaying her. I know – I'll tell the workers to drop a little extra corn and let Ruth pick it up. And I'll make sure no-one gives her any trouble.

Narrator While Ruth was working, Boaz went over to see her.

Boaz   What are you doing for lunch?

Ruth   Oh, don't worry about me. I'll just sit under the cedar tree to eat my bread and fruit.

Boaz   Well, I'd be very pleased if you'd come and have lunch with me.

Narrator Ruth was really pleased about that, and from then on she joined Boaz for lunch every day. They spent a lot of time together, and they soon realised that they were not 'just good friends', any more! Eventually, Boaz plucked up the courage to ask Ruth to marry him. Of course, she said, 'Yes!' because Boaz was a good, and kind man, and Ruth had come to love him very much indeed.

It was a wonderful wedding. Nearly everyone in Bethlehem came, and of course Naomi was given a special place among them. They sang and danced, and kept on drinking a toast.

- They *raised their glasses*
- They *shouted, 'To life!'*
- And then they *drank* every drop!

When it was all over, Ruth and Boaz settled down to begin their life together in his house. Before long, they had some more good news. Ruth was going to have a baby. Everyone was happy, and no-one more so than Ruth and Boaz. There again, perhaps there was one other person who was at least as happy as they were. Can you guess who that was?

Of course, it was Naomi. She was so happy she could hardly stand still – because she was going to be a grandma!

Biggest Isn't Always Best

Based on 1 Samuel 17

BEFORE THE DAY

Think of small things that are important: a fuse, a nail, a microchip. Which is bigger, a pound or fifty pence coin? Put together a display illustrating this principle.

Alternatively, prepare a large board, or some simple structure, with a doorway which only a very small child will get through.

• Think about the actions for all the children to join in during the story.

ON THE DAY

Introduction

We're going to hear a very famous story in a few moments, but first we'll say our 'Thank you' prayer.

'Thank you' Prayer

Thank you, God, for all you give us,
thank you for the earth and sea;
thank you, God, for special people,
thank you, God, for making me.

God's Story

Goliath had always been a bully. When he was a child, he used to take all the other children's toys – just to show how big and tough he was. His parents used to worry a lot, but were very pleased when he said he was going to join the army. His father said, 'That will make a man of him. He'll learn to do as he's told, and be polite to the people in charge.'

Then the army Goliath was in, the Philistines, went to war against the Israelites. But the Israelites didn't have anyone as big as Goliath, and everyone who tried to fight him got killed. Goliath used to enjoy showing off. Every morning, he went to the top of a hill, and shouted across to the Israelites: 'Send someone to fight me, if you can find anyone big enough. If he beats me, you will have won the war. Of course, if *I* win, *we'll* have won the war. Well, come on then, who's going to fight me?'

It was just like when he was at school – everyone was afraid of him, and he loved it!

One morning, a shepherd boy called David came to the Israelites' camp. David was very small – about a metre and a half in his sandals – but when he heard Goliath shouting, he thought, 'Someone ought to teach that big bully a lesson!' He went to the king, and said, 'I'll fight Goliath for you.'

Well, King Saul had never heard anything so funny! 'Oh yes?' he mocked. 'And what are you going to do – hit him in the kneecaps? Ho, ho, ho!' Well, it was true that David certainly was very small, compared with Goliath. But his father, Jesse, had always told his sons, 'Biggest isn't always best.'

'I'm a shepherd,' he said, 'And when lions and wolves attack the sheep, I drive them away. If God can help me fight a lion, he can certainly help me with Goliath.'

'Well, said the king, 'you'd better borrow my armour, to protect you. Come and try it on.'

Have you ever tried on a grown-up's clothes? Well, you can imagine how silly David looked and felt in the king's big, heavy armour. People couldn't help laughing at him. And when he tried to get the sword out and wave it, they all threw themselves about and roared with laughter. 'I'll make you sorry you laughed at me,' said David, as he took off the armour and marched out. What do you think he would use to fight Goliath?

• He couldn't use a *gun*,
     because they hadn't been invented
• Could he have used a *bow and arrow*?
• Could he have used a *dagger*?
• Or might he have used a *sword*?

David walked down to the stream, and chose five smooth stones for ammunition. Then he went out to meet Goliath.

'Now what have we here?' bellowed the giant. 'Are you the best that feeble lot could find? I'll feed you to the birds . . . I'll give you to the vultures for food . . . I'll . . .'

'Oh no you won't,' replied David, 'because God's going to help me.'

At that, the giant lost his temper, and aimed his spear at David. Quick as a flash, David put a stone into his sling, swung it round a few times and let go. The stone flew through the air, and hit the giant, bang in the middle of his forehead. He stopped for a moment, dropped his spear and sword, and then fell to the earth with a terrific crash. The ground shook so hard that people who weren't watching thought there'd been an earthquake!

All the Israelite army were very pleased with David. The Philistines weren't, of course – they got very frightened and ran away. They had learnt the hard way that 'biggest isn't always best'!

Our Story

Introduce the items on the display. If possible, involve the children. See whether they can suggest more small things that are special. What about themselves?!

Or, if using the alternative idea, call for volunteers to see who can get through the entrance. Ask them to imagine that they are trapped and someone has to go for help, or perhaps they're on a rescue mission. Who can get through the hole?

Prayers

We're Glad

Heavenly Father,
thank you for our friends,
who play with us and talk with us.
Thank you for people who care for us
and teach us,
and thank you for the fun we have together.
Thank you for the things we've done well
with your help.

We're Sad

Sometimes we're not nice to each other.
We get cross, we hurt each other,
we say things we shouldn't,
or sometimes we just don't notice
when someone needs help.
We're sorry,
and we'll try to do better in future.

Let's Pray for People

Loving Father,
it's easy to say that we trust you,
but we still get worried sometimes.
Help anyone who feels frightened,
or who is lonely.

Songs

Biggest isn't always best
God is making a wonderful world

– from *Wake up, World!*

God knows me
One more step, along the world I go

– from *Come and Praise*

Biggest Isn't Always Best

God's Story

Narrator   Goliath had always been a bully. When he was a child, he used to take all the other children's toys. No-one tried to stop him because he was so big, and they were all afraid of him. It wasn't that he really wanted the toys – he just wanted to show how big and tough he was.

Goliath   Come on, then, who's going to fight me?

Narrator   He grew up from a nasty young bully into an even nastier old one. Then he joined the Philistine army and went to war against the Israelites. The Israelites didn't have anyone as big as Goliath, and everyone who tried to fight him got killed. Goliath used to enjoy showing off. Every morning, he went to the top of a hill, and shouted his challenge across to the Israelites.

Goliath   Send someone to fight me, if you can find anyone big enough. If he beats me, you will have won the war. Of course, if *I* win, *we'll* have won the war. Well, come on then, who's going to fight me?

Narrator   One morning, while Goliath was shouting insults, a shepherd boy called David came to the Israelites' camp. David was very small – about a metre and a half in his sandals. But Goliath made him mad!

David   Someone ought to teach that big bully a lesson! I'll fight Goliath for you.

King Saul   Oh yes? And what are you going to do – hit him in the kneecaps? Ho, ho, ho!

David   You can laugh, but my mum says that biggest isn't always best. I'm a shepherd, and if God can help me chase lions away from the sheep, he can certainly help me with Goliath.

King Saul   Here, you'd better borrow my armour to protect you.

Narrator   Have you ever tried on a grown-up's clothes? Well, you can imagine how silly David looked and felt in the big man's armour. And when he tried to get the sword out and wave it, everyone threw themselves about and roared with laughter. David didn't think it was funny.

David   I'll make you sorry you laughed at me, and I don't need any silly bits of metal.

Narrator   I wonder what David would use to fight Goliath?

- He couldn't use a *gun*,
   because they hadn't been invented
- Could he have used a *bow and arrow?*
- Could he have used a *dagger?*
- Or might he have used a *sword?*

David didn't use any of those. He walked down to the stream, chose five smooth stones, and went to meet Goliath.

Goliath   Now what have we here? Are you the best that feeble lot could find? I'll feed you to the birds . . . I'll give you to the vultures for food . . . I'll . . .

David   Oh no you won't, because God's going to help me.

Narrator   At that, the giant lost his temper, and aimed his spear at David. Quick as a flash, David put a stone into his sling, swung it round a few times and let go. The stone flew through the air, and hit the giant, bang in the middle of his forehead. Goliath crashed to the ground, dead.

King Saul   I can't believe it! How can a little fellow like you beat a great big giant like him?

David   I told you – it's what my mum always says. Biggest isn't always best, you know.

Having a Whale of a Time

Based on the Book of Jonah

BEFORE THE DAY

Talk with the children about jobs they like to do, and jobs they try to get out of. Perhaps they could bring to school some illustrative objects. A simple display could be made up using, for example, a washing up mop labelled, 'Tracey doesn't like washing up'; a rolling pin marked, 'John enjoys baking cakes', etc.

• Think about the actions for all the children to join in during the story.

ON THE DAY

Introduction

Sometimes, God asks us to do things we don't like very much. We're going to hear a story about that in a moment, but first we'll say our 'Thank you' prayer.

'Thank you' Prayer

Thank you, God, for all you give us,
thank you for the earth and sea;
thank you, God, for special people,
thank you, God, for making me.

God's Story

Jonah was a fairly ordinary sort of chap – rather like people we know. He enjoyed looking after his garden, and chatting with his neighbours, but like many other people, there was something about him that really was not very nice. And we'll see what that was in a minute.

Jonah had often thought that he'd like to do something really special for God, and he used to daydream about the brave things he might do, or the important person he might become.

That's the thing about God, though – just when we think we've worked out what we'd like to do for him, he thinks of something different! So he told Jonah to take a message to Nineveh, a large town. The people there were living very badly – lying, stealing and fighting one another. In fact Nineveh was a bad place to be. So Jonah had to tell them to change, and start being good to one another, because otherwise, they would all end up being killed.

Jonah should have been pleased that God had such an important job for him – but he wasn't.

'Why should I go to Nineveh?' he thought. 'It's not in this country. They're all foreigners there – why should I help them?'

That was Jonah's bad point: he thought that anybody from another country was bad, and he only wanted to help his own people. 'After all,' he thought, 'there are plenty of people here who lie, and steal and fight. I should really go to them, not to some foreign place – charity begins at home!'

However, it was no good arguing with God who was determined to send Jonah to Nineveh.

'I know,' thought Jonah, 'I'll hide from God.' So he went down to the docks at a place called Joppa, and got on a ship to Spain.

Poor old Jonah didn't understand that you can't run away from God – but he was about to find out! When they got out to sea, a horrible storm began. The wind and waves were throwing the little ship about, while the thunder and lightning was frightening even the tough sailors! They were all wondering what they ought to do, and Jonah was getting frightened because he knew! Eventually, he did a very brave thing. He went to the captain, and said, 'It's all my fault. I'm running away from God. I-I-I think you'd better th-th-throw me overboard.'

'Good grief!' said the captain. 'What would your God do to us if we did a thing like that?'

Yet steadily the storm got worse, and the sailors got more frightened, until they decided to do what Jonah said. So over the side he went, with all the sailors praying like mad, asking God not to be angry! Straight away, the storm stopped. All the sailors were very pleased – but what about Jonah?

Of course, he tried to swim.

- He tried to do the *breaststroke*
- He tried to do the *crawl*
- He tried to do the *doggy paddle*

God hadn't forgotten Jonah, and he sent a very big fish, which opened its mouth and swallowed Jonah whole – which was a good thing, really! Imagine Jonah's surprise! 'Well!' he thought, 'I wonder how I get out of here.'

But he couldn't think of a way that he really fancied very much, so he decided to wait. Three days he was there. Can you imagine being shut up in a stuffy, smelly place for three whole days and nights? Still, it gave him a bit of time to think. He realised that hiding from God was silly, and decided to do what God wanted.

After three days, God got the fish to put Jonah back onto dry land near Nineveh. This time, Jonah did as God said. He walked right through the city, telling everyone to change before it was too late. And they listened to him. They stopped lying, and cheating, and fighting, and life became very good.

Jonah was cross about that, because he still didn't like the people he called 'foreigners'. But the only person whom that made unhappy was Jonah himself.

Isn't that a shame?

Our Story

Use the display to show that we all have to do jobs we don't like, but life's a lot happier if we do them cheerfully.

Prayers

We're Glad

Heavenly Father,
thank you for today:
thank you for the people we meet;
thank you for the things we do.
Thank you for the things we enjoy,
and thank you for being there
and helping us
at other times.

We're Sad

We would like to be friends with everybody,
but it's hard.
some people are not easy to like.
There again, we're sometimes difficult to like
as well!
But you still love us.
We're sorry we don't love people
the way you do.
Forgive us,
and help us to do better.

Let's Pray for People

Loving God, you love everybody.
You love us,
when we don't deserve it.
Bless those people we don't like,
and show us what is good about them.

Songs

I'm black, I'm white, I'm short, I'm tall
God made the earth
God is making a wonderful world
Pick up your feet and go!

– from *Wake up, World!*

Black and white
He's got the whole world in his hands
Somebody greater
God knows me

– from *Come and Praise*

Having a Whale of a Time

God's Story

Narrator   This is the story of Jonah. He was a fairly ordinary sort of chap, really – rather like people we know – but like many other people, then and now, there was something about him that really was not very nice. And we'll see what that was in a minute. Right now, God's about to spring a nasty surprise on Jonah.

God   Jonah, I've got a job for you.

Jonah   Oh, how exciting! What is it? D'you want me to rescue somebody from a dragon? Or is it a big famine somewhere that you need sorted out?

God   Oh, it's a lot simpler than that.

Jonah   Oh dear! How boring!

God   I just want you to pop along to Nineveh and give them a warning.

Jonah   What sort of warning?

God   Just that if they don't start behaving themselves better they're going to be in trouble.

Narrator   Jonah wasn't very pleased. He thought the people in Nineveh didn't deserve to be saved, because they were what he called 'forriners'. That was Jonah's weakness – he just couldn't believe that God cared about people in other countries.

Jonah   I don't think I really want to go to Nineveh. Why should I save all those nasty foreign people? I know, I'll go on holiday to Spain instead.

Narrator   So Jonah got on a ship and settled down for a long cruise, but then the most horrible storm began. Everyone was frightened, even the really tough sailors! And Jonah was even more frightened because he knew why it had happened. After a little while, he did a very brave thing. He went to see the captain.

Jonah   It's all my fault. I'm running away from God, and as long as I'm here, this storm's going to go on. I-I-I think you'd better th-th-throw me overboard.

Captain   Good grief! What would your God do to us if we did a thing like that?

Narrator   But the storm got even worse, and eventually they decided to do what Jonah said. So over the side he went, and as soon as Jonah hit the water, the storm stopped. All the sailors were very pleased – but what about Jonah? Of course, he tried to swim.

- He tried to do the *breaststroke*
- He tried to do the *crawl*
- He tried to do the *doggy paddle*

But the storm was too fierce. he got nowhere. Still, God hadn't forgotten Jonah, and he sent a very big fish, which opened its mouth and swallowed Jonah whole – which was a good thing, really!

Jonah   Well! Now what do I do? I can't think of a way out of here – or not one that I really fancy very much. I'd better wait and see what God's going to do next. And if he wants me to go and save those foreign people, then I suppose I'll have to go.

Narrator   When three days had gone by, God got the fish to put Jonah back onto dry land – not far from Nineveh. This time, Jonah did what God had wanted. He walked right through the city, telling everyone to change before it was too late. And the amazing thing is that they listened to him. They stopped lying, and cheating, and fighting, and life became very good indeed. But Jonah wasn't happy.

Jonah   I knew it! God's too soft. He's gone and forgiven all those nasty people, just because they changed. He should have given them what they deserved.

Narrator   The strange thing was that the only person who ended up unhappy was Jonah himself. Wasn't that a shame!

No Room

Based on Luke 2:1-7

BEFORE THE DAY

Ask the children to imagine moving to a smaller house. They will have to have a clear out. There will not be room for everything. What would they throw away? What would they make the effort to find room for? Discuss with them the reasons for their choices. Presumably the things they would discard would be those which they value least; we always find room for the important things. Ask them to bring to school something which they wouldn't mind losing, and something they would try hard to keep.

• Think about the actions for all the children to join in during the story.

ON THE DAY

Introduction

We're going to hear the Christmas story today, about how there was no room for Jesus at the hotel. First, we'll say our 'Thank you' prayer.

'Thank you' Prayer

Thank you, God, for all you give us,
thank you for the earth and sea;
thank you, God, for special people,
thank you, God, for making me.

God's Story

Simon and Susannah ran the local Bed and Breakfast, in Bethlehem. It wasn't very grand – just an ordinary house with a few extra rooms built on and a stable at the back. They had worked very hard to make it into a welcoming place to stay. The rooms were clean, each with a jug of water for washing, and another for drinking.

It wasn't just business – Simon and Susannah really wanted their visitors to be happy. They were very caring people, and

Simon never meant to be unkind. But there were times when he was, without meaning it – and this was one of them. So he was getting a good telling off from Susannah.

'D'you mean to tell me you turned that poor couple away, on a night like this,' Susannah shouted at him, 'and her expecting a baby any minute?'

'But, my love, we haven't any room,' said Simon.

That was true: people were sleeping in the passageways, and even on the dining room floor. They had to be up early each morning, before the other guests came down for breakfast. So you might think that Simon was quite right, but Susannah was still angry.

'Where there's a will, there's a way,' she said. 'I'm going to get that couple back here, and by the time I do, you'd better have thought of something.'

Susannah searched all over town. It wasn't easy, because the streets were crowded – people on donkeys, people walking, people carrying babies, some with children who didn't want to go where their parents were going, and said so. One little boy sat down in the road and refused to move, and people shouted at him to get out of the way. Susannah wanted to help, but she had to keep looking for the couple. Can you help her to look?

• She *looked to the left*
• She *looked to the right*
• She *turned her head from side to side*

Eventually, she saw them. She recognised the man straight away – tall, handsome, and worried looking! The couple, who turned out to be called Mary and Joseph, had been getting very worried, because Mary seemed likely to have her baby any minute!

'Don't worry,' said Susannah. 'I'm afraid that husband of mine is a bit silly sometimes, but he means well. You come with me. And if Simon hasn't thought of something by now, he'll be sorry!' So Susannah took them back to the house.

Simon was very pleased with himself. 'I still haven't got a room,' he said, 'but there's a shed out the back – not much in it, just a cow and some goats, so it smells a bit, but I'm afraid it's all there is.'

'It will have to do,' said Joseph. 'We're too tired to go on looking.'

So he gathered some straw together for Mary to lie on. Mind you, she didn't get a lot of sleep. The baby Jesus was born that night. Susannah stayed with Mary all night to help her. Simon was excited, too. He kept knocking on the stable door, calling, 'Has the baby arrived yet?' When Jesus was born, they realised there was nowhere to put him, where he could sleep.

'I know,' said Susannah. 'We could put some clean straw in that feeding trough.'

She pushed the animals out of the way, emptied the trough and put clean hay in it. Then she wrapped the baby Jesus in strips of cloth, to keep him warm, and put him in the trough. The animals weren't happy. They kept trying to get close to the manger. No-one was sure whether they were trying to see the baby or eat the straw! Eventually, Joseph tied them up to some hooks in the wall, and gave them some piles of hay to eat.

'There,' he said, 'that should keep them happy for a while.'

Suddenly, the shed seemed a lot nicer than it had before. Joseph and Mary had their new baby, and they were very glad indeed that they'd found somewhere in time!

Our Story

Show the items the children have contributed, and ask them to tell the rest of the group why they chose them. So how important are people? Surely, we should always make room for them?

Prayers

We're Glad

Thank you God,
for our homes;
for each other, for friends,
for people who think we matter.
Thank you for everything
that we share together

We're Sad

We think people are important, Jesus,
and we care about one another.
It's just that sometimes
we don't show it.
Sometimes we hurt people,
especially people we love.
We're sorry.

Let's Pray for People

Lord Jesus,
We pray for people who have no home,
who have no safe place to sleep;
people who don't feel loved
the way we do.
You know what it's like, Jesus.
Help us all to love one another
and make happy homes.

Songs

Born in a stable

– from *Wake up, World!*

Jesus Christ is here
Kum ba yah
Morning has broken
He was born in the winter

– from *Come and Praise*

There wasn't any room at the inn

– see *Appendix*

No Room

God's Story

Narrator   Simon and Susannah ran the local Bed and Breakfast, in Bethlehem. They were very caring people, and Simon certainly never meant to be unkind. But sometimes he did unkind things without meaning to – and this was one of them. So, not for the first time, he was getting a good telling off from Susannah.

Susannah   D'you mean to tell me that you turned that poor young couple away on a night like this – and her expecting a baby at any minute?

Simon   But we haven't any room, what else was I to do?

Susannah   Where there's a will, there's a way. I'm going to get that couple back here, and by the time I do, you'd better have thought of something.

Narrator   With that, Susannah went out into the night to look for the couple. Can you help her to look?

- She *looked to the left*
- She *looked to the right*
- She *turned her head from side to side*

And eventually she saw the couple. Their names were Mary and Joseph. They had been getting very worried, because it seemed as though Mary was about to have her baby any minute!

Susannah   Don't worry! I'm afraid that husband of mine is a bit silly sometimes, but he means well.

Mary   We don't want to be any trouble, but we really do need to find somewhere very soon.

Susannah No trouble at all. You come with me. And if Simon hasn't thought of something by now, he'll be sorry!

Narrator When they arrived, Simon was looking very pleased with himself

Simon I still haven't got a room, but there's a shed out the back – not much in it, just a cow and a couple of goats, so it smells a bit. But there's plenty of straw, and anyway, it's all there is.

Mary It will have to do. We're far too tired to go on looking.

Narrator So Mary got comfortable on a pile of straw, but she didn't get a lot of sleep. Just as she and Joseph had expected, their baby son, Jesus, was born that night. They realised there was nowhere to put him, where he could sleep. Then Susannah had an idea.

Susannah I know! We could put some clean straw in that feeding trough the animals are using.

Narrator The animals weren't happy. They kept trying to get close to the manger. No-one was sure whether they were trying to see the baby or eat the straw!

Susannah I think we'd better tie them up somewhere out of the way.

Narrator So that's what they did. The stable didn't seem quite so bad as it had at first, but I think I'd rather have my own nice warm home, wouldn't you?

Never Mind the Sheep, Look for the Baby

Based on Luke 2:8-20

BEFORE THE DAY

Shepherds were very special people, not only in the story of Jesus' birth but in everyday life for thousands of years. Think of all the things that needed to be made from wool before we had materials such as acrylic and plastic: clothes (woolly underwear as well as jumpers), tents, donkey bags, tapestries to cover walls, blankets and rugs to keep people warm in their beds, and so on. Draw pictures or collect items, and make a display.

Looking after the sheep was an important job – but was it fun? If anyone can bring some fleece into school, touch it and smell it – phew!

• Think about the actions for all the children to join in during the story.

ON THE DAY

Introduction

In a little while, we're going to hear a story about some shepherds. But first we'll say our 'Thank you' prayer.

'Thank you' Prayer

Thank you, God, for all you give us,
thank you for the earth and sea;
thank you, God, for special people,
thank you, God, for making me.

God's Story

Jed and Enoch were shepherds. And Jed was rather a grumpy one. He just wanted some excitement. 'Nothing ever happens,' he grumbled. 'It must be three weeks since we last had to chase a wolf away! And we can't even go into the town for a drink, because everyone tells us to go somewhere else.'

'Well,' said Enoch, 'you must admit that this isn't the cleanest job in the world.'

Jed was about to say something rude when he noticed that the sky was getting light. 'Wow!' he said. 'The night went quickly.'

But Enoch knew better. 'That's not the dawn,' he said. 'There's something funny going on.'

What happened next made Jed wish he'd never complained about being bored! There before his very eyes stood an angel. He was dressed in a robe, which shone so brightly that Jed thought the sun itself had come to life! Jed was terrified! What do you think he did?

- He *covered his eyes*,
  but he could still hear!
- He *covered his ears*,
  but then he could still see!
- So he *tried to do both at once*.
  But then he could see *and* hear!

Even Enoch was a bit flustered. 'Wh-wh-what d'you think we ought to do?' he asked. Talk about a silly question!

'Run like mad!' said Jed, 'What else!'

Then the angel said, 'Now, don't be silly; I'm not going to hurt you. I want to give you a message. Great news – about a special baby who's been born in Bethlehem. His name is Jesus, and he's going to save the world.'

By now, Jed had almost decided that a boring job like shepherding was just what he really wanted!

'Look,' said the angel, 'this will prove it to you. Go to Bethlehem, and look for a baby, wrapped in swaddling clothes, and lying in a cattle feeding trough.'

Just then, Jed said, 'Goodness me, there's thousands of them!'

And there were – angels, that is, not feeding troughs! The sky was full of angels, all singing and dancing, and having a real whoopee of a time! The whole sky was lit up like Corinth (which was the nearest thing they had to Blackpool in those parts) and it sounded as though all the choirs in the world had got together with a big amplifier! Then, all of a sudden, they'd gone! Just like that! The field was dark again, just as it had been before.

Enoch sat there for a time, rubbing his eyes and saying, 'It must had been a dream!' over and over again.

'Well if that was a dream, we must both have had one together,' said Jed. 'Anyway, there's only one way to find out – go to Bethlehem.'

'We can't do that,' Enoch protested. 'Who'll look after the sheep?'

'Never mind the sheep!' exclaimed Jed. 'We've got to look for the baby!' Jed was getting impatient. After all his complaining, something exciting was happening, and all Enoch could think about was counting sheep!

So they set off for the town, with Jed rushing on ahead, and Enoch following behind. When they got there, they hunted around and eventually found out where the baby was.

They ran across to the stable, and when they looked inside they saw a man, a woman and the baby. Just as the angel said, the baby was wrapped in swaddling clothes, and lying in the hay in the feeding trough.

The man, Joseph, noticed them, and invited them in. 'Look, Mary,' he said to his wife, 'we've got visitors.' Mary was very tired, but she smiled and welcomed the shepherds.

'We've come to see the baby,' said Enoch. 'What's his name?'

'We're going to call him Jesus,' said Mary, 'but do tell me – why have you come to see us?'

'Because an angel appeared, replied Jed, 'and told us that this baby was very special.'

'That's funny,' said Mary, thoughtfully, 'an angel said the same thing to me. I wonder what he meant.'

'I don't know,' said Joseph, 'but perhaps we'll find out when he grows up.'

Our Story

Draw attention to the woollen items in the display. Shepherds had a very important job to do, even if others didn't realise it. Are there other kinds of people like that today?

Prayers

We're Glad

Wonderful God,
how you surprise us!
Thank you for showing us
that we're all important,
even if we're not very grand!
Thank you!

We're Sad

We're sorry, God,
for ignoring people,
just because they seem unimportant to us.
Sometimes we forget
that people don't need to be grand
to matter to you.
We're sorry.

Let's Pray for People

God, our helper,
life can be so exciting,
but it can be so dull, as well!
Help people who are bored,
or fed up, like Jed was.
Show them something new,
something exciting,
something hopeful.
And show us how we can help, too.

Songs

Born in a stable
Out to the great wide world we go
– from *Wake up, World!*

Jesus Christ is here
– from *Come and Praise*

There wasn't any room at the inn
– see *Appendix*

Never Mind the Sheep, Look for the Baby

God's Story

Narrator	Jed and Enoch were shepherds. And Jed was rather a grumpy one – at least on this particular night.
Jed	It's no good, we've got to get out of this business.
Enoch	Oh yes? And what would you do instead?
Jed	I don't know what I want to do. All we do is sit out here all night, watching sheep, and we can't even go into the town for a drink, because the people all tell us to go away.
Enoch	Well, you must admit that this isn't the cleanest job in the world.
Narrator	Jed was about to make a rather rude reply when he noticed something strange. The sky was getting light.
Jed	Wow! The night went quickly!
Enoch	That's not the dawn. There's something funny going on.
Narrator	What happened next made Jed wish he'd kept his big mouth shut about being bored! There, before his very eyes, stood an angel. Well, I say 'stood' – 'hovered' might be a better word, because he didn't seem to have his feet on the ground – he was just, sort of, *there*! Jed was terrified! What do you think he did?

- He *covered his eyes*, but he could still hear!
- He *covered his ears*, but then he could still see!
- So he *tried to do both at once*.
  But then he could see *and* hear!

Enoch	Wh-wh-what d'you think we ought to do?
Jed	(*Aside, to audience*) Well! Talk about a silly question! (*To Enoch*) Run like mad! What else!

Angel	Now don't be silly, I'm not going to hurt you. All I want to do is give you a message. Great news – about a special baby who's been born in Bethlehem. His name is Jesus, and he's going to save the world.
Jed	I'm sorry I said life was boring. Can you make it boring again, please? I promise I won't complain any more!
Angel	I'll tell you what; this will prove it to you. Go to Bethlehem, and look for a baby wrapped in swaddling clothes and lying in a cattle feeding trough.
Enoch	Which feeding trough?
Jed	Goodness me, there's thousands of them!
Enoch	That's what I mean.
Jed	Not feeding troughs, you fool – angels!
Narrator	And so there were! The sky was full of angels having a real whoopee of a time! Then, all of a sudden, they'd gone! Just like that! The field was dark again, just as it had been before.
Jed	What do you think we should do?
Enoch	Now who's asking silly questions! Go to Bethlehem.
Jed	We can't do that! Who'll look after the sheep?
Enoch	Never mind the sheep! We've got to look for the baby! After all your complaining about life being boring, then at a time like this you want to count sheep!
Narrator	So they set off for the town. They found Joseph and Mary with their little baby, Jesus. And the baby, just as the angel said, was wrapped in swaddling clothes, and lying in the hay in the feeding trough.
Enoch	Perhaps now you'll stop moaning about life being dull!
Jed	Me? When did you ever hear me complain about that?

Ride That Camel! Chase That Star!

Based on Matthew 2:1-12

BEFORE THE DAY

Curiosity is a wonderful thing! Looking carefully at ordinary things, we can see aspects not noticed before. Get the children to look at flowers, leaves and anything else you can think of through magnifying glasses, and to draw what they see.

• Think about the actions for all the children to join in during the story.

ON THE DAY

Introduction

This morning, we're going to hear about some people who were very curious and who saw things that other people didn't notice. That's how they came to go on a very exciting journey. But first we'll say our 'Thank you' prayer.

'Thank you' Prayer

Thank you, God, for all you give us,
thank you for the earth and sea;
thank you, God, for special people,
thank you, God, for making me.

God's Story

Melchior, Caspar and Balthazar were wise men. They met together often to look at the stars and try to work out what they were about. They would sit around late at night (long after well-behaved children were asleep!) discussing whatever new star they had most recently seen.

One evening, Melchior got very excited. 'Look over there!' he shouted. 'There's a big new star.'

'Yes,' said Caspar, 'I wonder what it means.'

So Balthazar got the special books and looked it up. 'Let me see,' he said, ' "Star – extra bright . . ."' then he got really excited.

'It says here,' he told the others, 'that it means an important king has been born.'

'Right!' said Melchior. 'Let's go and find him.'

Everybody suddenly got very busy. Melchior called his servants, and said, 'Load up the camels. We'll need plenty of food, lots of water, changes of clothes, tents – and don't forget the first aid kit.' So everyone worked hard and, next night, they started off to follow the star – the wise men first and the servants behind with the luggage. How do you think they travelled?

• Would they *ride* on donkey's?
• Would they *drive* in a car?
• Would they *ride* on bicycles?

Of course, they rode on camels, didn't they? Sometimes it got very scary; they could hear wild animals howling, and some of the servants began to get nervous. But eventually, they saw a big city ahead.

'That should be Jerusalem!' said Balthazar. 'That's a capital city. So if we find the palace, we'll find the king.'

Now the king in Jerusalem was the wicked king Herod – and he got worried when he heard the wise men's story. 'A new born king?' he thought. 'I'm the king! There's not room for another one.'

Then one of his courtiers whispered to him, 'That sounds like the king the Bible speaks of – the great leader promised by God. He must be in Bethlehem'

'Well, then,' Herod whispered back, 'we'd better find him and get rid of him. Let's leave it to these people to find him for us.' He turned back to the wise men, and pretended to smile. 'I think the king you're looking for is in Bethlehem,' he said. 'When you've found him, would you tell me where he is, so that I can visit him, as well?'

Off went the wise men, and Herod turned to his courtiers and said, 'Right! When those silly men tell us where this so-called king is, we'll go and get him. King indeed!'

The wise men went to Bethlehem, and when they got there the star showed them exactly where the new king was. So they went in and found Mary and Joseph with Jesus.

'Hello,' said Melchior, 'I hope we're not disturbing you; my name is Melchior, and these are my friends, Caspar and Balthazar. We've come all the way across the desert to find your son.'

'Well,' said Mary, 'this is Jesus. He does seem to be causing a lot of excitement. We've had all kinds of visitors.'

Melchior went over to Jesus. 'We've brought you some presents,' he said. 'Look: gold, for a king.'

'But not just any king,' said Caspar, 'God's very special king. So I've brought some incense.'

'And I've brought you some myrrh,' Balthazar said. 'Being a king is hard, and you will have to suffer.'

Later, the wise men went away to their tents to sleep. 'We mustn't forget,' said Melchior, 'to call on that nice king Herod tomorrow, and tell him where Jesus is.'

But that night Melchior had a strange dream. An angel came to him and said, 'That "nice king Herod" as you call him is bad news. Whatever you do, don't tell him where the new king is, or there'll really be trouble.'

So the next day Melchior told the others, 'We're taking the pretty route home.'

'What about Herod?' said Balthazar.

'Shifty character,' said Melchior. 'Don't trust him a millimetre! I vote we give him a miss.'

'Good idea!' said Caspar. 'Let's go home.'

Our Story

Draw attention to the pictures which the class drew in preparation. See how much more they noticed when they really looked. Curiosity's 'in' and can lead the way to great discoveries!

Prayers

We're Glad

Dear God,
sometimes we have to make an effort:
search for what we want,
think about things, work things out.
That's why you gave us eyes, and brains.
Help us to use them,
and make us thankful that we've got them.

We're Sad

We're sorry about being lazy.
We're sorry about the things we miss,
that you're trying to show us, or tell us.
We're sorry for the times
when we couldn't be bothered to think,
to try to understand
what you were saying.
Forgive us,
make us more curious, more interested.

Let's Pray for People

Loving God,
we pray for people who are sick,
and can't go out,
people who can't walk very well,
people who can't see and hear
the wonderful things in the world.
Show us if there are ways
we can help them,
so that they will know
what a good world this is.

Songs

I'm black, I'm white, I'm short, I'm tall
In the winter, nights are dark
Keep on travelling on!

– from *Wake up, World!*

Morning has broken
Black and white

– from *Come and Praise*

Ride That Camel! Chase That Star!

– see *Appendix*

Ride That Camel! Chase That Star!

God's Story

Narrator	Melchior, Caspar and Balthazar were three wise men. They used to meet together often to talk about important things, and to look at the stars. They would sit around, very late at night (long after well-behaved children were asleep!) discussing whatever new star they had most recently seen. One evening, Melchior got very excited.
Melchior	Look over there! There's a great big star that I've never seen before. I wonder what it means.
Balthazar	I'll look it up. Let me see, 'Star – extra bright . . .' Hey, it says here that it means a special king has been born, and the star will lead us to him.
Melchior	Then what are we waiting for? Let's go and follow it.
Narrator	Everybody suddenly got very busy, packing the things they would need, and by the next night, when the star appeared again, they were ready to go. How do you think they travelled?

- Would they *ride* on donkeys?
- Would they *drive* in a car?
- Would they *ride* on bicycles?

Of course, they would ride on camels, wouldn't they?

Balthazar	Come on everyone, let's get moving! The three of us will ride ahead and the servants follow behind with all the food and water and camping kit – and I hope you've remembered to pack the kettle.
Narrator	They travelled through the desert for many weeks, moving at night when they could see the star, and sleeping in their tents during the day. Eventually, they saw a big city ahead.
Melchior	Where are we?

Caspar	According to my reckoning that should be Jerusalem.
Balthazar	Good, that's a capital city. Let's find the palace.
Narrator	Now this was definitely a bad idea. The king in Jerusalem was the wicked king Herod – and he got a bit worried when he heard what the wise men wanted.
Herod	*(Aside, to audience)* I'm the king! There's not room for another one. I'd better find him and get rid of him.
Narrator	So Herod did a bit of checking up, and then went back to the wise men.
Herod	I think the king you're looking for is in Bethlehem. When you've found him, would you let me know, so that I can go to see him, as well?
Narrator	So off went the wise men, and Herod turned to his courtiers and started making plans.
Herod	Right! When those silly men come back and tell me where this so-called king is, I'll have him killed. King indeed!
Narrator	The wise men went to Bethlehem, and found Mary and Joseph with Jesus. They had some presents for the baby.

- *Gold*, for a king.
- *Frankincense*, for God's special king.
- *Myrrh*, for his suffering.

Then they went to their tents to sleep. And next morning they got ready to leave for home.

Balthazar	We mustn't forget to stop and tell that nice king Herod where Jesus is.
Melchior	I don't think so. I've found out that 'that nice king Herod' as you call him is bad news.
Caspar	I knew it! Shifty character! Don't trust him a millimetre! I vote we give him a miss.
Melchior	Good idea! Let's go home the pretty way.

The Man Nobody Wanted

Based on Matthew 8:1-4

BEFORE THE DAY

Ask the children about their phobias. For example: are they afraid of spiders? But spiders are actually very good, because they eat flies and other germ-spreading insects. Perhaps they could draw pictures, or cut them out from magazines, comics etc. and make a display.

• Think about the actions for all the children to join in during the story.

ON THE DAY

Introduction

Sometimes we're afraid of things and people for silly reasons, and we don't see how good they are. We'll think about that in a minute. But first we'll say our 'Thank you' prayer.

'Thank you' Prayer

Thank you, God, for all you give us,
thank you for the earth and sea;
thank you, God, for special people,
thank you, God, for making me.

God's Story

Joe was very unhappy. He hadn't got friends, or a home, or a job. In fact, he had nothing, apart from the clothes he was wearing. And they weren't very nice – well, they wouldn't be, since he never got the chance to change them!

It hadn't always been like that. Joe used to have lots of friends. And he had a very nice home, too – his father was a farmer, and Joe used to enjoy life on the farm, watching the crops grow, and helping look after the animals. Everyone liked Joe, and he was often invited to parties and dances. But that was before his illness.

Joe developed a nasty skin disease. No-one's sure exactly what it was, but it looked horrible! Everyone was afraid of catching it from him; so they told him to go away. Grown-ups stopped their children playing with him and taught them to be afraid of him, too. They used to stand a long way away and shout nasty things at him, and if he came a bit too near they would start throwing stones. Can you imagine what else they might have done?

• They might *put out their tongues*
• They might *shake their fists*
• They might *pull horrible faces*

Joe really thought that no-one loved him. He was terribly sad.

Even his parents were afraid.

'I'm sorry Joe, but you can't stay here,' his father said. 'We don't want the family catching it, too, whatever it is. You'll have to go and live in the caves just outside the town.'

'Don't worry,' said his mother, 'we'll bring you food every day.'

So Joe had to leave home and live right away from other people. His parents took him food, but it wasn't enough. They were afraid to touch him, and what Joe wanted more than anything else was to be hugged!

Then he heard about a man called Jesus who could work miracles. 'Well,' he thought, 'if people were nice to me, that would be a miracle!' So he went looking for Jesus.

Joe wasn't very hopeful. Everyone else drove him away, so why shouldn't Jesus just do the same? But he thought it was worth a try.

What a surprise he had! Jesus didn't drive him away. In fact, he stopped what he was doing and went to meet him. Well! That was different for a start! 'Hello,' he said, 'is there something I can do for you?' Joe was amazed!

'Aren't you afraid of me?' he asked. 'Don't you want to call me names and send me away?'

'Now why on earth would I want to do that?' asked Jesus.

'Everyone else does,' replied Joe, 'and you must admit I look pretty horrible!'

'But that's only on the outside,' said Jesus.

Then he did the most wonderful thing. He walked right up to Joe, looked him in the eyes and took hold of his hand! 'Wow!' thought Joe. 'No-one's ever done that before – not since I got my skin disease.'

He was so excited that at first he didn't realise that Jesus had started speaking to him again. 'Now that I've touched you,' said Jesus, 'other people will, too. They won't be afraid of you any more. Go into the town, and people will be nice to you.'

It was then that Joe realised that his skin disease had gone. His skin was as smooth and healthy as it had been when he was a child! Joe was very, very happy. He went back to the farm and showed his parents. They were overjoyed and threw their arms around him. Now he could live at home again, and have what he really most wanted – love and company.

Life was good again for Joe. He met up with his old friends again, children stopped being nasty to him, and he even got a job. But most of all, he felt loved and wanted. And all because of a man called Jesus, who reached out and touched him when nobody else would.

Our Story

Draw attention to the display. Can the children think of people of whom others are afraid, and who feel left out because of it?

Prayers

We're Glad

Thank you God for lots of things, especially happiness. Thank you for fun and the funny things that happen, (especially . . .) Thank you for laughter. Thank you for loving us.

We're Sad

God, sometimes bad things happen: sometimes we get hurt; sometimes we hurt other people. often we hurt you. We're sorry, God. Thank you for loving us, even then.

Let's Pray for People

Thank you God for people we love, and who love us, (especially . . .) Please look after them. Thank you for all our friends and our family; help us to love one another more. Help us to be specially kind to those whom nobody seems to want.

Songs

Jesus had all kinds of friends
I'm black, I'm white, I'm short, I'm tall
God is making a wonderful world
Out to the great wide world we go!

– from *Wake up, World!*

God knows me
He's got the whole world in his hand

– from *Come and Praise*

Thank you, O God, for all our friends

– see *Appendix*

The Man Nobody Wanted

God's Story

Narrator This is a story about a man nobody wanted. We're going to call him Joe. He hadn't always been treated that way. Joe's family were farmers, and Joe used to enjoy life on the farm. Everybody liked him, and he was often invited to parties and dances. But that was before his illness.

Joe developed a very nasty skin disease. No-one's really sure exactly what it was, but it looked horrible! Everyone was afraid that if he came near them they would catch it from him. So they told him to go away. Grown-ups stopped their children playing with him and taught them to be afraid of him. Can you imagine what else they might have done if he came towards them?

- They might *put out their tongues*
- They might *shake their fists*
- They might *pull horrible faces*

Jo thought no-one loved him. He was terribly sad. Even his parents were afraid.

Joe's Dad I'm sorry Joe, but you can't stay here. We don't want the family going down with it, too, whatever it is. You'll have to go and live in the caves just outside the town.

Joe's Mum Don't worry, we'll see you don't starve. We'll bring you food every day and leave it outside the cave.

Narrator So Joe had to leave home and live outside the town, right away from other people. His parents were terribly upset, but they couldn't think of anything else to do. They kept their word and took him food, but it wasn't enough. What Joe wanted more than anything else was to be hugged!

Then he heard about a man called Jesus, who could work miracles. So he went looking for Jesus, and what a surprise he got!

Joe Er, excuse me, Jesus . . .

Jesus Hello, how nice to see you. Is there something I can do for you?

Joe Aren't you afraid of me? Don't you want to call me names and send me away?

Jesus Now why on earth would I want to do that?

Joe Everyone else does, and you must admit I look pretty horrible!

Jesus But that's only on the outside.

Narrator Then Jesus did the most wonderful thing. He walked right up to Joe, looked him in the eyes, reached out and took hold of his hand!

Joe Wow! No-one's ever done that before – not since I got my skin disease.

Jesus Now that I've touched you other people will, too. They won't be afraid of you any more. Go into the town and people will be nice to you.

Narrator It was then that Joe realised that his skin disease had gone. His skin was as smooth and healthy as it had been when he was a child! Joe was very, very happy. Life was good again for Joe. He went back home, and his parents were overjoyed! He met up with his old friends again, children stopped being nasty to him, and he even got a job. But most of all, he felt loved, and wanted. And all because of a man called Jesus, who reached out and touched him when nobody else would.

The Man Who Came in Through the Roof

Based on Mark 2:1-12

BEFORE THE DAY

Ask the children to imagine they can't use their arms or legs. What would they be unable to do? More importantly, what would they still be able to do? They could make a chart, using headings such as, 'I can't . . .' and 'But I can . . .' Perhaps most importantly in the 'But I can . . .' column, they could still think and listen. Could you arrange for someone who represents disabled people to come and take part in the assembly?

• Think about the actions for all the children to join in during the story.

ON THE DAY

Introduction

Today, we're going to think about how Jesus treated disabled people. But first we'll say our 'Thank you' prayer.

'Thank you' Prayer

Thank you, God, for all you give us,
thank you for the earth and sea;
thank you, God, for special people,
thank you, God, for making me.

God's Story

Barney was a very wise and clever man who lived in a town called Capernaum with his wife, Sarah. Everyone came to Barney if they had a problem, and he would listen very carefully and ask a lot of questions. Very often, he didn't need to give advice, because he asked such good questions that people thought of the answers for themselves. People liked Barney, because he cared and understood.

Then Barney became ill. He couldn't use his arms and legs any more. The silly thing was that, although his brain was still perfectly alright, just because he couldn't walk people thought he couldn't do anything at all. So they all stopped asking him for help. And when friends visited Barney, they used to talk to Sarah, about him, instead of talking to him. If they made him a drink, they would turn to Sarah and say, 'Does he take sugar?' They seemed to think that just because his legs wouldn't work, neither would his brain. What silly people!

You can understand why Barney was frustrated. Just think of some of the things he couldn't do for himself and some of the things he still could do:

- He couldn't *use a knife and fork*
- and he couldn't *comb his own hair*
- But he could *watch*
- and he could *listen*
- and he could *talk*
- and he could *think*

Sarah got very unhappy because she could see how hurt Barney was, but Barney was also worried about Sarah. 'I must be an awful problem to you,' he would say. This upset Sarah because although, looking after Barney wasn't easy, she loved him and did it willingly.

Then one day, Barney heard that Jesus was in town. 'Now there's someone who could help!' he thought. 'Sarah,' he called, 'can you find out where Jesus is?' Sarah did better than that. She came back with four of Barney's friends: Paul, Nick, Joe and Ben.

'We've found Jesus,' said Ben, 'and we'll take you to him.' They picked him up on his mattress and carried him out of the door! Through the town they hurried, down alleyways and along main streets, until they arrived at a house with a huge crowd gathered outside.

'This is the place,' said Paul, 'but how can we get in?' 'I know,' said Ben, 'if we go up onto the roof, we can remove some tiles and lower him through the hole.'

'I suppose it might work,' said Nick 'Paul, go and get some rope.'

Inside the house, everyone was listening to what Jesus was saying when all of a sudden they noticed noises coming from overhead. Then the tiles were pulled off and Nick's bearded face appeared. 'I'm terribly sorry about this,' he said, and then to everybody's amazement a mattress appeared and started to come down. Jesus got up and went over, to see Barney lying on the mattress and looking very embarrassed!

'I'm sorry about this,' Barney said. 'I'm afraid we have damaged your friend's roof.'

'Well,' said Jesus, 'I think my friend will get it fixed quite easily.'

'I really am sorry about the way I look,' said Barney, 'but my friends were so eager I didn't even get time to change my clothes, or have a shave.'

'Don't feel guilty,' said Jesus, 'feel good about yourself – God loves you!'

The people around were horrified. 'He's got no right to say that,' they said. 'Only God can tell us not to feel guilty!' At this Jesus got very impatient.

'What silly people you are!' he exclaimed. 'No wonder this man's friends were so desperate!' Then he turned to Barney and said, 'Why don't you roll that thing up and carry it home with you?' Then he took Barney's hand and lifted him up. Barney was amazed to find strength in his legs again. His friends were excited, and Sarah was overjoyed! Barney thanked Jesus, and his friends, and hugged and kissed Sarah. Then he went home. People were very surprised to see him walking – so surprised that they actually talked to him, instead of to Sarah! By the time he got home, he'd made four appointments with people who wanted advice! Life was looking good again, for Barney and Sarah!

Our Story

Refer to the 'I can't . . .' and 'I can . . .' charts, and see if the larger group wants to add anything to it. Emphasise the positive things which disabled people can do. If you have managed to get a special speaker, this is the time to invite them to join in.

Prayers

We're Glad

Thank you, God, for our strength,
for all the things we can do,
without needing help,
and for all the ways
in which we can help one another.
(Most of all we enjoy . . .)
Thank you, God, very much.

We're Sad

Dear God, sometimes we hurt people
without meaning to,
by trying too hard to be kind.
Sometimes we act as though people are stupid,
just because they can't walk, or can't hear.
Help us to remember that there are lots of things
we can't do.
Help us to be polite, and thoughtful
to those we call 'disabled'.

Let's Pray for People

Loving God, there are all kinds of people
sharing the same world.
Some are very strong, some are very brainy,
some are very good at making things,
some paint, or draw, or write, or sing,
some can listen and think.
Everyone's good at something.
Help us *all* to be good
at being kind!

Songs

Pick up your feet and go!
God is making a wonderful world
Keep on travelling on!
Out to the great wide world we go!

– from *Wake up, World!*

One more step along the world I go
When I needed a neighbour

– from *Come and Praise*

Thank you, O God, for all our friends

– see *Appendix*

The Man Who Came in Through the Roof

God's Story

Narrator Barney was a very wise and clever man who lived with his wife, Sarah. If anyone had a problem, Barney would listen very carefully and be really helpful. Then Barney became ill. He couldn't use his arms and legs any more. He had to spend all day lying on his bed.

Barney Just because I'm paralysed, people treat me like a fool. Old Mrs. Wossname talks about me as if I wasn't there: (*mockingly*) 'Does *he* take sugar?' I ask you!

Sarah They're very silly, but they mean well. Anyway, I've heard that Jesus is coming to town. Perhaps he can help.

Barney Oh, Jesus is much too important to bother with people like me. How you put up with me I don't know.
   You can understand why Barney was frustrated.

- He couldn't *use a knife and fork*
- He couldn't *comb his own hair*
- But he could *watch*
- and he could *listen*
- and he could *talk*
- and he could *think*

And Sarah used to get really upset when he said he was a burden to her.

Sarah Barney, I like looking after you. Now I won't hear any more arguments; I'm going to get you to Jesus if I have to carry you there myself!

Narrator But Sarah didn't need to do that. She went and found four of Barney's friends and brought them back to the house. The four men picked up Barney's mattress, with him still on it, and carried him out of the door!

Barney   Hey, hang on a minute! I'm not dressed properly.

Sarah   Don't be silly! D'you think Jesus cares what you look like?

Narrator   Well, it was no good Barney protesting any more, because by now they were halfway down the street. But when they got to the house, there was such a crowd that they couldn't get in.

Sarah   We're not giving up now, are we, lads? Get up on the roof and get some slates off, and Barney can 'drop in' on Jesus.

Narrator   Inside the house, the people were startled when all of a sudden the tiles were pulled off the roof and a mattress started to come down. Jesus got up and went over to find Barney looking very embarrassed!

Barney   I'm ever so sorry about this. I'm afraid we have damaged your friend's roof. And I'm really sorry about the way I look, but . . .

Jesus   I do wish you'd stop feeling so guilty. Feel good about yourself – God loves you just as you are!

Narrator   Some of the people around were horrified! They thought only God could tell people not to feel guilty! 'Ooh,' they said, 'what a cheek!'

Jesus   *(Very impatiently)* Oh you are silly people! No wonder Barney's friends were so desperate! Look, Barney, why don't you get off that thing, roll it up and carry it back home with you?

Narrator   Barney was amazed to find strength in his legs once more. He thanked Jesus, and his friends, and hugged and kissed Sarah. Then he walked home. People on the way actually talked to him instead of to Sarah and he'd soon made four appointments with people who wanted advice! Life was looking good again for Barney and Sarah!

Rain, Rain, Go Away

Based on Mark 4:35-41

BEFORE THE DAY

Talk about the weather! Ask the children what kind of weather they like best. Why do we need rain? Perhaps they could either draw pictures or bring in examples of different clothes for different weather.

• Think about the actions for all the children to join in during the story.

ON THE DAY

Introduction

We're going to think about the weather in a few moments. But first we'll say our 'Thank you' prayer.

'Thank you' Prayer

Thank you, God, for all you give us,
thank you for the earth and sea;
thank you, God, for special people,
thank you, God, for making me.

God's Story

Jesus decided it was time to go home. It had been a long, hard day, and he was tired. He knew his friends were tired, too. The trouble was, they had to get across to the other side of Lake Galilee. So they had quite a journey ahead of them. 'Come on,' he said to his disciples, 'let's go home.'

So they got into the boat and pushed off into the lake. Peter was a little uneasy. He knew that storms could start suddenly on the lake, and their boat was not very big. So he told the rest of the disciples to keep a good look-out.

'You go up to the front, Andrew,' said Peter, 'and Thomas, you go to the back and keep a special watch on those clouds just over the hills – I don't like the look of them!' (I expect Peter would actually have said, 'bow' and 'stern', normally, but not all the disciples were used to being in boats, so he made it easy for them.)

'Well,' said Jesus, 'I think I'll just go and lie down in the back of the boat.' And it wasn't long before he was fast asleep.

'What do those clouds look like, Thomas?' asked Peter.

'Not very good,' replied Thomas. 'They're very black, and they're coming this way.'

'Right!' said Peter. 'Philip, you and James get that sail down, or the wind will turn us right over. Judas and John, make sure all the heavy boxes are tied down; and everyone else, sit down, and hang on tight!' He'd hardly got the words out before a sudden wind hit the boat, and blew it out towards the middle of the lake. It whipped up the waves until they were as high as houses, and the little boat was being tossed around on the top of the sea. Some of the waves came over the side, and the boat began to fill with water.

• The boat was rocking *from side to side*
• and rocking *backwards and forwards*
• and all the time, Jesus was *sleeping*!

Everyone was very frightened indeed. Everyone, that is, except Jesus who was still fast asleep in the back. 'Well! Look at that!' said Thomas. 'We're working like mad to keep the boat afloat, and he's just lying there, sleeping!'

Peter went over to Jesus and shook him. 'Look,' he said, 'the boat's likely to sink any minute, and you're just lying there. Don't you care if we die?'

Jesus got up and went to the front of the boat. There he shouted to the wind and the sea. 'Stop it!' he said. 'Be quiet.'

Peter was about to say, 'Well, a fat lot of good that will do!' when he noticed that it had gone quiet. And the boat had stopped rocking. And it wasn't filling with water any more. He tried to speak, but was so amazed that he just stood there, with his mouth open, looking for all the world like a fish! Jesus went over to him and put his hand on his shoulder. 'Why are you all so afraid?' he asked. 'Didn't you trust me?'

'Wh-wh-what's going on?' stammered Peter.

'Who is this man?' asked Andrew.

'I can't believe it!' said John. 'Even the wind and the sea do as he tells them!'

Jesus smiled, and quietly went to sit in the back of the boat again until they all got to the shore. 'There!' he said. 'Now we can *all* get some sleep!'

Our Story

Use the display to talk about the effects of different kinds of weather, and how we have to prepare for it. It's good that we've got good clothes and safe homes. Some people aren't so lucky, so how can we show that Jesus cares about them?

Prayers

We're Glad

God, our friend,
you give us all kinds of weather,
and all of it's good for someone.
Thank you for all of it:
for rain, for sun, for snow, for clouds.
And thank you for our home,
and our food.

We're Sad

Loving God, we're sorry
that we can't always be good.
We try very hard, but it isn't easy.
If we've hurt other people,
help us to make it right.

Let's Pray for People

Dear God,
some people don't like it hot,
others complain when it's cold.
Some people like the sun,
others are happy when it's raining.
Some people are ill, or tired,
and get upset easily.
Help them to be happy,
and let them know you love them
whatever the weather's like.

Songs

Out to the great wide world we go

– from *Wake up, World!*

He's got the whole world in his hand
Morning has broken
Who put the colours in the rainbow?
Kum ba yah
God knows me

– from *Come and Praise*

Sing a song of weather

– see *Appendix*

64

Rain, Rain, Go Away
God's Story

Narrator   Jesus decided it was time to go home. It had been a long, hard day and he was tired. He knew his friends were tired, too; and they had quite a journey ahead of them to get across to the other side of Lake Galilee.

Jesus   Come on folks, let's go home!

Narrator   So they got into the boat and pushed off into the lake. Peter was a little uneasy. He knew that storms could be dangerous on that lake.

Peter   You go up to the front. Andrew, and Thomas, you go to the back. And keep a special watch on those clouds just over the hills – I don't like the look of them!

Jesus   Well, I think I'll just go and lie down in the back of the boat and get a bit of sleep.

Peter   What do those clouds look like, Thomas?

Thomas   Not very good; they're very black, and they're coming this way.

Peter   Right! Philip, you and James get that sail down, or the wind will turn us right over. Judas and John, make sure all the heavy boxes are secure; and everyone else, sit down, and hang on tight!

Narrator   He'd hardly got the words out before a sudden wind hit the boat, and blew it out towards the middle of the lake. It whipped up the waves until they were as high as houses, and the little boat was being tossed around on the top of the sea. Some of the waves came over the side, and the boat began to fill with water. Everyone was very frightened indeed. Everyone except Jesus, that is.

- The boat was rocking *from side to side*
- and rocking *backwards and forwards*
- and all the time, Jesus was *sleeping*!

Thomas was the first to notice.

Thomas Well! Look at that! We're working like mad to keep the boat afloat, and he's just lying there, sleeping!

Peter Hey! Jesus! Wakey wakey! The boat's likely to sink any minute, and you're just lying there. Don't you care if we die?'

Narrator Jesus got up and went to the front of the boat. There, he shouted to the wind and the sea.

Jesus Stop it! Be quiet!

Peter Well, a fat lot of good that will do! – Hey, why's it all gone quiet?

Narrator Would you believe it! The boat had stopped rocking. And it wasn't filling with water any more. Peter was so amazed that he just stood there, with his mouth open, looking for all the world like a fish!

Jesus Why are you all so afraid? Didn't you trust me?

Peter Wh-wh-what's going on?

Thomas Who is this man? Even the wind and the sea do as he tells them!

Jesus Well, that's that! Close your mouth, Peter, before you swallow a flying fish, and get us back home. Then we can all get some sleep.

Wake Up, Little Girl

Based on Mark 5:22-43

BEFORE THE DAY

Think about having fun! What kind of things do the children enjoy doing? Perhaps they can draw some pictures, or maybe they have some photographs of themselves at fairgrounds or theme parks.

• Think about the actions for all the children to join in during the story.

ON THE DAY

Introduction

We're going to hear shortly about a little girl who really enjoyed life. But first we'll say our 'Thank you' prayer.

'Thank you' Prayer

Thank you, God, for all you give us,
thank you for the earth and sea;
thank you, God, for special people,
thank you, God, for making me.

God's Story

Jairus was a very important man in the synagogue, but he wasn't bossy. He was always kind to everybody, and so he had lots of friends in the town.

Jairus was married to Susie, and they had a daughter called Hannah aged about twelve. Just like other children, Hannah loved to play and explore with her friends. If there was a tree in sight Hannah would climb it, and if not she'd find something else. She was very energetic. She was also very caring. She would never hurt anyone, and was most upset if anyone was unhappy. Hannah had lots of friends as well.

One day Hannah didn't seem very well. She just sat indoors, and when her friends asked her out, she said, 'Not today, thank you; I think I'll just have a quiet day at home.'

'You never have quiet days at home,' said Susie. 'Are you ill?'

'I'm all right!' snapped Hannah. 'Why can't you leave me alone?' And what do you think she did next?

- She *clenched her fists*
- She *screwed up her face*
- She *waved her fists in the air*

And she stamped off to her room, leaving Susie standing with her mouth open in amazement.

When Jairus came in, Susie said, 'I'm terribly worried about Hannah. She's been really unwell all day. And this afternoon she actually shouted at me.'

'You're joking!' said Jairus. 'Hannah never shouts at anybody.'

'I'm *not* joking,' replied Susie. 'Hannah shouted at me, stamped her foot, and went off to her room, and she hasn't come out since.'

Jairus knocked on the door of Hannah's room and went in. Straight away, he knew she was ill. So Susie hurried out to the doctor's surgery and soon came back with the doctor. He went into Hannah's room. After a few moments, he came out. 'I'm afraid Hannah's very ill,' the doctor explained, 'and there's nothing I can do. What she needs is a miracle.'

After the doctor had left, Jairus and Susie sat beside Hannah's bed, and racked their brains trying to think of anyone else who could help them. 'Of course!' Susie said. 'We know someone who can work miracles.'

'Yes,' said Jairus, 'Jesus works miracles. But some people at the synagogue have been very unkind to him.'

'Jesus is too good a person to say 'no' just because of that,' said Susie. So Jairus went to look for him.

Jairus hunted everywhere, until he found Jesus. 'Please help me,' he gasped. 'My daughter's very ill.'

Jesus smiled at him. 'You'd better show me,' he said, 'and don't worry – she'll be all right.'

But then one of Jairus's neighbours arrived. 'I'm terribly sorry, Jairus,' she said, 'but it's too late. Don't bother Jesus now – I'll take you home.'

'What do you mean, "Too late"?' asked Jesus. 'With God, it's *never* too late! Don't worry Jairus, I said she'd be all right, and I don't break my promises.'

When they got to the house, it was full of people crying because Hannah was dead. Jesus asked them to leave. 'I don't know what he thinks he can do,' someone mumbled. 'I know a dead person when I see one.' But they went. Jesus went over to Hannah's bed, and took her hand.

'Get up, little girl,' he said. And to the great amazement and joy of Susie and Jairus, Hannah's eyes opened.

'Hello,' she smiled, 'who are you?'

'My name's Jesus,' answered Jesus. 'What's yours?'

'Hannah,' she replied, 'and it's nice to meet you.'

Jairus and Susie rushed over to hug Hannah, who liked that very much, but wasn't really sure what was going on. 'Are you really all right?' asked Susie.

'Yes, Mother, of course I am,' answered Hannah, kindly. 'What on earth's the matter?'

'We can't thank you enough, Jesus!' Susie said.

'It was my pleasure,' said Jesus, 'but you'd better give her something to eat.'

Hannah looked very surprised. 'Eat?' she said. 'No time for that! It's a beautiful day – can't I go out to play?'

Our Story

Jesus understood Hannah – because he loves to enjoy life, as well! Draw attention to the display, and talk about how good God wants life to be for everybody.

Prayers

We're Glad

Thank you, Jesus,
for wanting us to be happy.
It's good to be alive,
especially when people love us
and care about us.
Help us to love life even more!

We're Sad

Forgive us please, Jesus,
for the times we've hurt people.
Sometimes, we've spoiled things,
made life hard for them,
because we've been selfish.
Whenever someone needs you,
you want to help them.
Help us to do the same.

Let's Pray for People

Let's pray for people who don't enjoy life.
Some people are lonely,
or perhaps they're ill.
Maybe they knew someone who has died.
Even when they're sad,
help them to know that life's worth living,
and help us to show them
that you care.

Songs

God made the earth
Out to the great wide world we go

– from *Wake up, World!*

God knows me
He's got the whole world in his hand
Morning has broken
Kum ba yah

– from *Come and Praise*

Wake Up, Little Girl
God's Story

Narrator Jairus was a very important man in the synagogue. He was married to Susie, and they had a lovely daughter called Hannah aged about twelve. One day, Hannah didn't seem very well.

Hannah I was going out to play, but I think I'll just have a quiet day at home.

Susie You never have quiet days at home. Are you ill?

Hannah *(Angrily)* I'm all right! Why can't you leave me alone?

Narrator And what do you think she did then?

- She *clenched her fists*
- She *screwed up her face*
- She *waved her fists in the air*

And then she stamped off to her room, leaving Susie standing with her mouth open in amazement. A bit later, Jairus came home.

Susie I'm terribly worried about Hannah. She's been really unwell all day. And this afternoon, she actually shouted at me.

Jairus You're joking! Hannah never shouts at anybody.

Susie I'm *not* joking. Hannah shouted at me, stamped her foot, and went off her room, and she hasn't come out since.

Narrator Jairus knocked on the door of Hannah's room and went in. Straight away, he knew she was ill. So Susie hurried out and came back with the doctor, who hurried in to see Hannah.

Doctor I'm afraid Hannah's very ill, and there's nothing I can do. What she needs is a miracle.

Susie	Of course! We know someone who can work miracles.
Jairus	Yes, Jesus does. But some people at the synagogue have been very unkind to him.
Susie	Jesus is too good a person to say 'no' just because of that.
Narrator	Jairus hunted everywhere, until he found Jesus. But just as he was explaining about Hannah, one of his neighbours arrived and said it was too late. Jesus didn't agree.
Jesus	What do you mean, 'Too late'? With God, it's *never* too late!
Narrator	When they got to the house, Jesus asked them to leave, and then went over to Hannah's bed and took her hand.
Jesus	Get up, little girl.
Narrator	Then, to the amazement of Susie and Jairus, Hannah's eyes opened, and she sat up!
Hannah	Hello, who are you?
Jesus	My name's Jesus. What's yours?
Hannah	Hannah, and it's nice to meet you.
Narrator	Jairus and Susie rushed over to hug Hannah, who liked that very much, but wasn't really sure what was going on.
Susie	Are you really all right?
Hannah	(*kindly*) Yes, Mother, of course I am. What on earth's the matter?
Susie	Jesus, we can't thank you enough!
Jesus	It was my pleasure. But you'd better give her something to eat.
Hannah	(*Looking very surprised*) Eat? No time for that! It's a beautiful day – can't I go out to play?

What a Catch!

Based on Luke 5:1-11

BEFORE THE DAY

Ask the children to talk about days when things have gone really well, and when they haven't. You could make a display of their own pictures or stories about such days.

• Think about the actions for all the children to join in during the story.

ON THE DAY

Introduction

We'll hear a story about Jesus and his friends soon. But first we'll say our 'Thank you' prayer.

'Thank you' Prayer

Thank you, God, for all you give us,
thank you for the earth and sea;
thank you, God, for special people,
thank you, God, for making me.

God's Story

Simon and his brother Andrew, who were fishermen, had been fishing all night on Lake Galilee but caught nothing. 'It's your fault, Simon,' claimed Andrew. 'You took us to the wrong part of the lake.'

'Rubbish!' shouted Simon. 'You didn't bait the nets properly.'

'Don't blame me!' said Andrew. 'I've always done well when you haven't been with me.' Simon was getting angry. He was really a very kind man, but he sometimes said and did things without thinking first and he was about to suggest they give up fishing altogether. Luckily, before Simon spoke, Andrew noticed something strange.

'Look,' he said, 'there's a crowd gathering over there. Isn't that Jesus, the carpenter, talking to them?'

'That's right,' said Simon. 'He's mended our boat a few times. I wonder what he's doing here.'

Jesus had stopped working as a carpenter, and was going around the towns and the countryside telling people about God. When Simon and Andrew saw him, he was getting a bit worried; the crowd were pushing to get close to him and, without meaning to, pushing *him* into the water!

'Hey, Jesus!' shouted Simon. 'You'd better get into our boat unless you want your feet washed!'

Jesus got into the boat, which the brothers pushed out a little way from the bank. Then Jesus could speak to the crowd without being pushed into the lake. Meanwhile, Andrew and Simon carried on tidying the boat and forgot about their argument – especially when they started to listen to what Jesus was saying.

Afterwards, Jesus said, 'Simon, why not go out a little bit further and see if you can catch anything?'

'No point,' said Simon. 'We've fished all night and caught nothing. I was looking forward to a rest.'

'The way you fish,' said Andrew, 'you'll get plenty of rest.'

'Don't start that again,' said Jesus. 'I heard you before, when I was trying to teach. Come on, put the boat out, and see what you find.'

'Well,' said Simon, 'there's nothing there, but if you say so, I'll have another go.'

'I do say so, Simon,' said Jesus. So Andrew hoisted the sail, Simon untied the rope from the shore, and soon they were sailing out into deep water.

When they got a little way out, Simon said, 'Where do you think we should try, Jesus?'

'Oh, just a bit further on yet,' Jesus answered. A few minutes later, he said, 'Try here, Simon.'

All this time, Simon was thinking, 'Blooming cheek! I don't tell him how to make chairs! Why should he tell me where to fish?' But he didn't say it, partly because he didn't want to hurt Jesus, and partly because Jesus had a strange way of being right, although how he did it was a mystery! So Simon and Andrew threw the net over the side and almost immediately the boat lurched over.

'We've snagged the net on something,' Simon called to Andrew.

'We can't have done,' Andrew shouted back. 'The water's too deep.'

'Then, we've caught a whale!' Simon replied.

What they had caught was the biggest catch of fish they'd ever seen! The net was brimming over, and Simon decided they'd better get the net in before it broke.

'We'll never do it,' said Andrew, huffing and puffing as he pulled at the net. Can you help them?

- Come on now: *Pull!*
- *Pull!*
- *Pull!*

It was no good, and Simon had almost given up when he noticed James and John sailing nearby. He raised his voice. 'Hey, James, over here – give us a hand!' James and John realised that the other boat was in trouble and came to help. They held the net between the two boats and got it to the shore.

'How did you get all those fish?' John asked. 'We'd just tried there and got nothing!'

'I don't know,' said Simon. 'Let's just say that as carpenters go, Jesus is a good fisherman.'

Our Story

Sometimes things go well, and sometimes they don't. Life's like that. Use the display to illustrate the point and remind the children that sometimes even the professionals need a few lessons!

One word of caution: Be careful not to appear to say that if we listen to Jesus things always go well! Plenty of people have found out the hard way that it's not as simple as that!

Prayers

We're Glad

Thank you, Jesus, for everything good
that happens to us,
especially when we don't expect it!
Thank you for helping us to get things right,
and thank you for giving us
people who help us, as well.
Thank you, Jesus.

We're Sad

Not everything goes well, Jesus.
Sometimes people are disappointed.
Perhaps we could be more helpful,
to each other, or to other people.
We're sorry if we let anyone down.
Please forgive us.

Let's Pray for People

Let's pray for people in very important jobs,
who dare not make mistakes:
people like doctors and train drivers,
nurses and airline pilots, *(and . . .)*
Please, Jesus, be helpful to people
who have important jobs.
Help them not to make mistakes,
and if they do, forgive them,
and help them to forgive themselves.

Songs

One hundred and fifty three
Out to the great wide world we go

– from *Wake up, World!*

All things bright and beautiful
Who put the colours in the rainbow?

– from *Come and Praise*

What a Catch!
God's Story

Narrator Simon and his brother Andrew, who were fishermen, had been fishing all night on Lake Galilee, but caught nothing.

Andrew It's your fault, Simon. You took us to the wrong part of the lake.

Simon Rubbish! You didn't bait the nets properly.

Andrew Don't blame me! I've always done well when you haven't been with me.

Narrator Simon was getting angry. He was really a very kind man, but he sometimes said and did things without thinking first. But before he could answer Andrew noticed something strange.

Andrew Look, there's a crowd gathering over there. Isn't that Jesus, the carpenter, talking to them?

Simon That's right, he's mended our boat a few times. I wonder what he's doing here.

Narrator Jesus had stopped working as a carpenter, and was going around telling people about God. When Simon and Andrew saw him, he was getting a bit worried, because the crowd were pushing to get close to him, and, without meaning to, pushing him into the water!

Simon Hey, Jesus! You'd better get into our boat unless you want your feet washed!

Narrator Jesus got into the boat, which the brothers pushed out a little way from the bank. Then Jesus could speak to the crowd safely. Meanwhile, Andrew and Simon carried on tidying the boat, and forgot about their argument.

Jesus Simon, why not go out a little bit further, now I've finished teaching, and see if you can catch anything?

Narrator	So they hoisted the sail and went out into deeper water.
Simon	Where do you think we should try, Jesus?
Jesus	Oh, just a bit further on yet.
Simon	*(Aside, to audience)* Blooming cheek! I don't tell him how to make chairs! Why should he tell me where to fish?
Jesus	Sorry, Simon, I didn't quite catch that.
Simon	Oh! Er . . . I said it's very kind of you to show us where to fish, Jesus.
Jesus	Yes, of course . . . I think we should try here, Simon.
Narrator	So Simon and Andrew threw the net over the side and almost immediately the boat lurched over.
Simon	We've snagged the net on something.
Andrew	We can't have done, the water's too deep.
Narrator	They had caught so many fish that they couldn't haul the net into the boat. Can you help them?

- Come on, now: *Pull!*
- *Pull!*
- *Pull!*

Andrew	It's no good, we'll need more help, Simon. Isn't that James's boat over there?
Simon	Hey, James, over here – give us a hand!
Narrator	James came over, and they held the net between the two boats and got it to the shore.
James	Well, Simon, How did you get all those fish? My brother and I had just tried there and got nothing!
Simon	I don't know. Let's just say that as carpenters go, Jesus is a good fisherman.

The Soldier Who Believed in Jesus

Based on Luke 7:1-11

BEFORE THE DAY

Think about great people who are (or were) of religions other than Christianity. For example, the Mahatma Gandhi followed what many would see as 'the way of the cross' and many children will know the name of Lionel Blue who, while a committed Jew, values very highly some insights and traditions of Christianity.

Perhaps the children could do some simple research about the faith symbols of other cultures and either model or draw some of them for a display.

• Think about the actions for all the children to join in during the story.

ON THE DAY

Introduction

In a minute, we're going to hear about a man who trusted Jesus, even though he didn't follow him. But first we'll say our 'Thank you' prayer.

'Thank you' Prayer

Thank you, God, for all you give us,
thank you for the earth and sea;
thank you, God, for special people,
thank you, God, for making me.

God's Story

Marcus was an officer in the Roman army, and he had a servant called Septimus who looked after him. Normally, Roman soldiers were hard men and the Israelite people hated them, but no-one hated Marcus.

'You know,' said Septimus one day, as he was hanging up Marcus's tunic, 'since you built them that synagogue, they love you even more than before.'

'I didn't do it for that,' said Marcus. 'I just don't see why we have to be cruel to people whom we've beaten in war. They're good people and I like them.'

'But they never come to visit us,' said Septimus.

'They can't,' Marcus replied. 'They have a law against it. A lot of them think it's silly, but they still have to obey it.'

One day, Septimus fell ill. The army doctor said he was dying. Marcus was very upset; Septimus was more like a friend than a servant. All Marcus could think of to do was go to the market and buy him some figs to cheer him up. Jud, the fig merchant, said, 'Is Septimus ill?'

'I'm afraid he's dying,' said Marcus, sadly.

'I know who could help him,' said Jud. 'There's a man called Jesus who's always healing people. He's probably in the main square.' With that, Jud ran off leaving his stall with nobody watching it.

'It's no good,' said Marcus. 'He won't be able to go into the house.' But Jud was out of earshot. Marcus turned to Nathan the carpet seller at the next stall and said, 'But from what I've heard, he doesn't need to come; all he has to do is say the word. Nathan, could you go after Jud, and take this message? I'll look after your carpet stall.' Marcus wrote a note, and Nathan ran off with it.

Meanwhile, Jud had found Jesus talking with some friends under a palm tree. He went running up to Jesus, frantically trying to attract his attention.

• He *waved his arms in the air*
• He *snapped his fingers*
• He *pointed towards the market place*

'Sir! Sir!' he shouted. 'Come quickly – someone's dying.'

'Who's dying?' asked Jesus.

'Septimus is,' said Jud. 'He's the servant of a Roman centurion called Marcus.'

Jesus set off straight away to find Marcus, with Jud leading the way. Before they had got very far, Nathan came running up, panting for breath. 'Thank goodness I've found you!' he spluttered. 'I'm too old for this kind of thing.'

Here, read this.' Jesus took the note from him, and this is what it said,

Dear Jesus,
Please don't come to my house. I'm a soldier, and not of your religion. I know all about giving and obeying orders. I tell people to 'Come here,' and they do. I say, 'Go there,' and they do. So I know that if you just say the word, Septimus will be well again.

Yours sincerely,

Marcus

Jesus read the note aloud, and then turned to his friends.

'Did you hear that?' he asked them. 'This man is not of our religion, he doesn't worship with us, and he doesn't say the same kind of prayers as we do. But he's got a lot more faith than most people of our own religion have. I've never heard anything like it before – not even in Israel!'

Then Jesus said to Nathan, 'Go and tell Marcus that Septimus is better.'

Nathan went off like a rocket, with Jud just behind. When they arrived, Marcus was just leaving the market to go home.

'I've had a message from home,' he said. 'Septimus is better! What do you think of that?'

'Wonderful!' said Nathan, but there was one little thing worrying him. 'D'you know what else the healer said?' he asked.

'No,' said Marcus.

'Well,' said Nathan, thoughtfully, 'he said that you had more faith than any of us. And you don't even believe in our religion.'

'Really!' said Marcus. 'What a strange thing to say!' But he didn't stop to think about it. He was too eager to get home and see Septimus again.

Our Story

Show the children the items and/or pictures in the display, and point out that we know lots of really good people who aren't followers of Jesus, and who either don't worship at all or who do so very differently.

Prayers

We're Glad

You know what people are like, Jesus.
You know that sometimes
we surprise each other.
Thank you for nice surprises,
thank you for making life so exciting!

We're Sad

We're sorry, Jesus,
for the times when we're unfair to people.
Just because they're different from us,
we think that they can't do things,
or that we shouldn't trust them.
Sometimes that makes them sad.
Help us not to be prejudiced.

Let's Pray for People

Loving God,
we pray for people who are different,
and who get left out.
Help us to realise that, to some other people,
we are the ones who are different.
We wouldn't like to be left out because of that.
Help us to be kind.
And help us to see that wonderful people
come in all shapes, sizes and colours!

Songs

I'm black, I'm white, I'm short, I'm tall
Jesus had all kinds of friends

– from *Wake up, World!*

Black and white
Morning has broken
God knows me
He's got the whole world in his hand
One more step

– from *Come and Praise*

The Soldier Who Believed in Jesus
God's Story

Narrator Marcus was an officer in the Roman army, and he had a servant called Septimus. Normally the Israelite people hated Romans, but no-one hated Marcus – as Septimus reminded him one day.

Septimus D'you know, sir, since you built them that synagogue, they love you even more than before.

Marcus I didn't do it for that. I just don't see why we have to be cruel to people whom we've beaten in war. They're good people and I like them.

Narrator One day, Septimus fell ill. The army doctor said he was dying. Marcus was very upset; he went to the market and buy him some figs to cheer him up. Jud, the fig merchant, thought it was strange for Marcus to do his own shopping.

Jud Is Septimus ill?

Marcus I'm afraid he's dying.

Jud I know who could help him. There's a man called Jesus who's always healing people. He's probably in the main square.

Marcus It's no good; he won't be able to go into the house, since I'm not a Jew.

Narrator But Jud was out of earshot. He'd gone running off without even getting anyone to watch his stall for him.

Marcus But from what I've heard, he doesn't need to come; all he has to do is say the word.

Narrator Marcus wrote a note, and got Nathan, a carpet seller, to take it to Jesus. Meanwhile, Jud had already found him. He went running up to Jesus, frantically trying to attract his attention.

- He *waved his arms in the air*
- He *snapped his fingers*
- He *pointed towards the market place*

Jud   Sir! Sir! Come quickly – someone's dying.

Jesus   Who's dying?

Jud   Septimus is. He's the servant of a Roman centurion.

Narrator   Jesus set off straight away to find Marcus, with Jud leading the way. Before they had got very far, Nathan came running up and gave Jesus Marcus's note.

Jesus   It says: *Dear Jesus,*

                 Please don't come to my house. I'm a soldier, and not of your religion. But I know that if you just say the word, Septimus will be well again.

                 Yours sincerely, Marcus

                 Did you hear that? This man is not of our religion but he's got a lot more faith than most people of our own religion have. I've never heard anything like it before – not even in Israel! Jud, go and tell Marcus that Septimus is better.

Narrator   Jud and Nathan went off like a couple of rockets. When they arrived, Marcus was about to go home.

Marcus   I've had a message from home: Septimus is better!

Jud   Wonderful! The healer said a really funny thing, though.

Marcus   What was that?

Jud   Well, he said that you had more faith than any of us.

Marcus   Really? What a strange thing to say! But do excuse me – I can't wait to get home and see Septimus again.

A Very Unhappy Person

Based on Luke 8:43-48

BEFORE THE DAY

Discuss with the children the subject of illness and the reasons for it. They can draw pictures of themselves and write labels 'Amy with chicken-pox', 'David's broken leg'. Why did these things happen to them?

Who makes us better? Remember sometimes people don't get better for a long time and living with an illness can be very hard.

• Think about the actions for all the children to join in during the story.

ON THE DAY
Introduction
We're going to hear shortly about a very special miracle Jesus performed. But first we'll say our 'Thank you' prayer.

'Thank you' Prayer
Thank you, God, for all you give us,
thank you for the earth and sea;
thank you, God, for special people,
thank you, God, for making me.

God's Story
At one time, Anna was very happy. She had a husband, Abe, who loved her very much, and two sons, John and David, who thought that she was the best mum in the world. Abe had a good job at the local quarry which was providing stone for the new army barracks. That meant that Abe had plenty of work and John and David would probably get good jobs, too. Everything looked good, until Anna got ill.

'Go and see the doctor,' said Abe. 'We can afford to pay.' In those days, you had to pay the doctor every time you went, but Anna wasn't worried, 'It won't be anything serious,' she thought.

The doctor came and examined her.

• He asked her to *put out her tongue (Ugh!)*
• He *checked her pulse*
• He asked her to *say 'Ah'*

And then he said, 'Hmm . . . I'm not too sure about this. You'd better see a specialist.'

'I don't mind that,' said Anna. 'How much will it be?'

'Well, said the doctor, 'that depends. The local one has a long waiting list, but I know someone in Jerusalem who's very good, and he could see you more quickly. The only trouble is, he costs more, and of course, there's the camel fare.'

'I'll go to him,' said Anna.

And she did. But he couldn't help her either, and sent her to somebody else. Well, this went on for a long time, and eventually Abe said, 'I'm sorry, but we can't afford any more doctors.'

'I'll just have to accept it,' said Anna. Then she began to think, 'It must be me – I must be a bad person, and God doesn't want me to get better.' So she decided just to put up with it. She and Abe became very unhappy, but they tried not to let John and David see it.

When she heard that Jesus was in town, she could hardly believe her luck! Surely, *he* could heal her! She put on her best clothes and went out to meet him. But then she became very nervous.

'What if I was right?' she wondered. 'What if I'm a bad person, being punished? He's obviously a holy man – I'd better not trouble him.' Then an idea came to her. 'If he's so wonderful, perhaps I don't need to ask him. Perhaps I could just touch his coat,' she thought. So she crept up behind him, and touched just the edge of it.

It worked! She was better already! But then a really frightening thing happened. Jesus stopped. And he turned round. And he asked, 'Who touched me?'

Peter, one of his friends, laughed. 'Look,' he said, 'there are people all around you, pushing and shoving, and you ask who touched you!'

'Yes,' said Jesus, 'and I want to know.'

He obviously wouldn't take 'no' for an answer. So Anna plucked up her courage and went to him.

'I touched you,' she said. 'I'm sorry if you're cross, but I'm ill and no-one can help me, and I thought that if I . . .' Then she stopped, because she had noticed that the look in Jesus' eyes was really kind.

'Don't apologise,' he said. 'Do you feel better?'

'Oh, yes!' she exclaimed. 'Heaps and heaps better!'

'Good,' said Jesus. 'That's because you had faith. But you should never have been afraid; no matter how bad you think you are, you can always face me.'

Anna was over the moon! Touching Jesus' coat had cured her illness. But actually meeting him, had made her feel good about herself again. She went dashing home to tell Abe about it. Abe saw her running up the garden path and nearly died from shock!

'How long have you been able to do that?' he asked.

'About ten minutes!' laughed Anna, and gave him an enormous hug.

Life was good again. Anna could enjoy being with Abe and the boys, without the worry her illness had caused; she never thought bad things about herself again, and she always remembered a man called Jesus who had changed her life.

Our Story

Divide the display board or OHP acetate into two columns, headed: 'God wants us to be . . .' and 'God doesn't want us to be . . .' Then ask the children to fill in the columns. Try to encourage the children to think in terms of health and happiness, rather than ethics! Point out that God doesn't want anyone to feel ill or guilty. There may be many reasons why illness happens, but God's punishment isn't one of them!

Prayers

We're Glad

Jesus, it feels good,
knowing people love us,
and especially
knowing you love us.
Thank you for loving us,
and thank you for showing it
by giving us each other.

We're Sad

Jesus you loved people,
even when others didn't.
Sometimes we find it hard
to love people.
Sometimes we hurt them,
make them feel guilty.
We're sorry.

Let's Pray for People

Jesus, some people feel bad
because they're ill,
or because they feel ashamed.
Some people think no-one loves them
and that they must be bad.
Jesus, be a friend to them
And help us to be friends to them, too.

Songs

She was sick and she needed healing
Jesus had all kinds of friends
I'm black, I'm white, I'm short, I'm tall

– from *Wake up, World!*

All things bright and beautiful
God knows me
He's got the whole world in his hand

– from *Come and Praise*

Thank you ,O God, for all our friends

– see *Appendix*

A Very Unhappy Person

God's Story

Narrator At one time, Anna was very happy. She had a husband, Abe, who loved her very much, and two sons, John and David, who thought that she was the best mum in the world. Everything looked good, until Abe noticed that Anna seemed to be ill. Now in those days you had to pay whenever you wanted to see a doctor.

Abe I'm worried about you, Anna. I think you should go and see the doctor – we can afford to pay.

Anna I think you're right – but I don't expect it will be anything serious.

Narrator So Anna went to see the doctor, and he examined her.

- He asked her to *put out her tongue (Ugh!)*
- He *checked her pulse*
- He asked her to *say 'Ah'*

Doctor Hmm . . . I'm not too sure about this. You'd better see a specialist.

Anna I don't mind that. How much will it be?

Doctor Well, that depends. The local one has a long waiting list, but I know someone in Jerusalem who could see you more quickly. The only trouble is, he costs more.

Anna I'll go to him – I don't want the illness to get worse while I'm waiting.

Narrator And that's what she did. But he couldn't help her either, and sent her to somebody else. And it all cost Abe and Anna an awful lot of money.

Abe I'm sorry, but we can't afford any more doctors. I don't know what we're going to do now.

Anna	I'll just have to accept it. It must be me – I must be a bad person, and God doesn't want me to get better.
Narrator	Now we know how silly that is – God doesn't want anybody to be ill. But Anna was very unhappy, until she heard that Jesus was in town. She could hardly believe her luck! Eagerly she went out to meet him. But then she became very nervous.
Anna	What if I'm a bad person, being punished? I'd better not trouble him. *(Pause)* I know! If he's so wonderful, perhaps I don't need to ask him. Perhaps I could just touch his clothes.
Narrator	So Anna crept up behind Jesus, and touched just the edge of his coat. It worked! She was better already! But then a really frightening thing happened. Jesus stopped. And he turned round. And he spoke.
Jesus	Who touched me?
Narrator	Now that sounded silly! People all around him were pushing and shoving, and he asked who touched him!
Jesus	Yes, and I want to know.
Anna	I touched you. I'm sorry if you're cross, but I'm ill and no-one can help me, and I thought that if I . . .
Jesus	Don't apologise! Do you feel better?
Anna	Oh, yes! Heaps and heaps better!
Jesus	Good. That's because you had faith. But you should never have been afraid; no matter how bad you think you are, you can always face me.
Narrator	Anna was over the moon! Touching Jesus' coat had cured her illness. But actually meeting him, had made her feel good about herself again. From that day onwards Anna always remembered a man called Jesus who had changed her life.

'Sunday Trading'

Based on Luke 13:10-17

BEFORE THE DAY

Talk about rules and why we need them in order to live peacefully together in our schools and communities. Find lots of examples and write them down on cards. What is the most important rule of all that Christians try to follow? It is to love each other. In trying to keep to all the other rules, and making others keep to them we can sometimes forget this first and most wonderful rule.

Tell the children about the woman in the story, and ask them to draw 'before and after' pictures of her.

• Think about the actions for all the children to join in during the story.

ON THE DAY

Introduction

In a few moments, we're going to hear about Jesus healing someone, but not everybody was pleased about it. First, though, we'll say our 'Thank you' prayer.

'Thank you' Prayer

Thank you, God, for all you give us,
thank you for the earth and sea;
thank you, God, for special people,
thank you, God, for making me.

God's Story

Rachel had been ill for eighteen years! It was a strange illness that made it impossible for her to stand up. She had been to lots of doctors, but no one had helped, and she looked like being bent double for the rest of her life. It was a great shame, because she had been very fit, going for long walks, swimming, and even taking part in the annual 'Donkey Derby'! Now, even simple things like hanging out the washing were impossible because she couldn't reach the line. Even though she wasn't particularly old, life seemed to have lost all meaning. She longed to walk upright like other people, and perhaps play with the children. Even looking up to see the sky was an effort.

In those days, Saturday was rather like the Christian Sunday. People went to the synagogue to worship God, and no-one was allowed to do any unnecessary work. They were very strict about that – really, rather too strict. Of course, it was good for almost everyone to rest on the same day, because it meant that life was quieter. So everybody was happy with that. The trouble was that the strict laws sometimes got silly. This particular day, Jesus was teaching in the synagogue and he saw Rachel come in, bent double and obviously in pain. So he went to help.

'What's the matter?' Jesus asked. 'Can't you stand up straight?'

'I haven't stood up straight for eighteen years!' replied Rachel. 'And even if I could I'd keep my head down in this place.'

'Why?' asked Jesus.

'Well,' said Rachel, 'women don't have much of a place in the synagogues do we? Even if I could stand straight, I'd be frightened to, in case someone noticed me!'

'That's silly,' said Jesus. 'Everyone should be able to hold their head up in God's house.'

And he took her by the hand and lifted her up. It was amazing! Her back straightened, and she looked right into Jesus' eyes! Everyone was amazed, and some were pleased. But at least one person wasn't. Jerry, the synagogue leader was angry. He *said* he was cross with Jesus for 'working' on the Sabbath day, but some people thought that he just didn't like Jesus and was trying to catch him out.

'You've broken the law,' he said. 'You've worked on the rest day.'

'Oh, really!' said Jesus. 'I simply took her hand and helped her to stand up straight. Don't you want her to stand up straight in God's house?'

'That's not the point,' said Jerry. 'You're a healer – so healing is work, and you shouldn't work on a rest day.'

Jesus thought this was very silly and cruel. 'What if she was a farm animal and fell into a well?' he asked. 'Would it be alright to pull her out?'

'That's different,' shouted Jerry, getting very angry. 'That's an emergency.'

'So,' said Jesus, 'farm animals are more important than women!' Everyone laughed at that – except Jerry, who just got angrier, because people like that hate being laughed at!

What do you think Jerry did?

- He *waved his arms about*
- He *shook his fist*
- He *pulled horrible faces*

Jesus went on, and said, 'You can feed and rescue animals on the rest day, so of course a woman who's put up with illness for eighteen years should be freed from it on the same day! She's just as important as you or anyone else, and don't you forget it.'

Jerry had no answer to that, and was very embarrassed. Everyone else was overjoyed. 'That was the best service we've had for a long time,' someone said – and that just made Jerry jump up and down all the more!

As for Rachel, she went home, singing and dancing, looking up at the beautiful sky, and stopping to play with every child she met on the way. From now on, life was going to be very different indeed!

Our Story

Have a large board with LOVE EACH OTHER written on it and say that this is the most important rule God gives us. Then ask for ideas for other rules we need in order to live peacefully together. You could use the school rules. The children who have those rules written on smaller cards can come up and pin them over the original rule. By the end it is almost totally obscured. (This can work effectively on an OHP). Now wipe the rules away to reveal again the most important message, explaining that this is what Jesus does.

Prayers

We're Glad

Loving God,
thank you for caring for us,
and for showing us
the best way to live.
Thank you for telling us
to care for one another,
and giving us rules
to keep us safe.

We're Sad

We're sorry, Jesus,
for our selfishness.
We're sorry if anybody has been hurt,
because we've been too fussy.
Forgive us and help us to remember
that the most important rule
is to love each other.

Let's Pray for People

Jesus, our friend,
be a special friend to all those who are in prison.
Help them to know that you love them,
and that we are praying for them.
And help us to be kind to people we know
who get into trouble.

Songs

I'm black, I'm white, I'm short, I'm tall
Jesus had all kinds of friends
Out to the great wide world we go!

– from *Wake up, World!*

One more step along the world I go
When I needed a neighbour

– from *Come and Praise*

Stand Up! Walk tall in the house of God!

– see *Appendix*

'Sunday Trading'

God's Story

Narrator Rachel had been ill for eighteen years! It was a strange illness that made it impossible for her to stand up. She had been to lots of doctors, but no one had helped, and she looked like being bent double for the rest of her life. It was a great shame, because she had been very fit, going for long walks, swimming, and even taking part in the annual 'Donkey Derby'! Now, even simple things like hanging out the washing were impossible because she couldn't reach the line.

In those days, Saturday was rather like the Christian Sunday, but the law was much stricter – so strict that it sometimes got silly. This particular Saturday, Jesus was teaching in the synagogue. He saw Rachel come in, bent double, and he went to help.

Jesus What's the matter? Can't you stand up straight?

Rachel I haven't stood up straight for eighteen years! And even if I could, I'd keep my head down in this place.

Jesus Why?

Rachel Well, women don't have much of a place in the synagogues do we? Even if I could stand straight, I'd be frightened to, in case someone noticed me!

Jesus That's silly! Everyone should be able to hold their head up in God's house.

Narrator Jesus took Rachel by the hand and lifted her up. It was amazing! Her back straightened, and she looked right into Jesus' eyes! Everyone was amazed, and some were pleased. But at least one person wasn't. Jerry, the synagogue leader was angry. He *said* he was cross with Jesus for 'working' on the Sabbath day, but some people thought that he just didn't like Jesus and was trying to catch him out.

Jerry	You've broken the law; you've worked on the rest day.
Jesus	Oh, really! I simply took her hand and helped her to stand up straight. Don't you want her to stand up straight in God's house?
Jerry	That's not the point. You're a healer – so healing is work, and you shouldn't work on a rest day.
Jesus	What if she was a farm animal and fell into a well? Would it be alright to pull her out?
Jerry	That's different. That's an emergency.
Jesus	So, farm animals are more important than women!
Narrator	Everyone laughed at that – except Jerry, who just got angrier, because people like that hate being laughed at! What do you think Jerry did?

- He *waved his arms about*
- He *shook his fist*
- He *pulled horrible faces!*

But Jesus ignored him and went on speaking.

Jesus	You can feed and rescue animals on the rest day, so of course a woman who's put up with illness for eighteen years should be freed from it on the same day. She's just as important as you or anyone else, and don't you forget it!
Narrator	Jerry had no answer to that, and was very embarrassed. Everyone else was overjoyed. Someone even said that it was the best service she'd been to for a long time – and that just made Jerry jump up and down all the more!
	As for Rachel, she went home, singing and dancing, looking up at the beautiful sky, and stopping to play with every child she met on the way. From now on, life was going to be very different indeed!

Jesus and the Tax Man

Based on Luke 19:1-10

BEFORE THE DAY

Ask the children how their first impressions of others are formed. Is it by their clothes, their dress, their colour, their accent? How do they react to someone who wears a uniform for their job, like a traffic warden or a priest. Have they ever been wrong about people?

Could they make up some stories (or write down true ones) about people being misunderstood because of prejudice?

You might also make something, if you wish, of the last line spoken by 'Spectator' in the drama.

• Think about the actions for all the children to join in during the story.

ON THE DAY

Introduction

We're going to hear the story of Jesus and the Tax Collector in a moment. But first we'll say our 'Thank you' prayer.

'Thank you' Prayer

Thank you, God, for all you give us,
thank you for the earth and sea;
thank you, God, for special people,
thank you, God, for making me.

God's Story

In this story, Jesus meets a man called Zacchaeus. Zacchaeus was a small man – the kind who can easily get lost in a crowd. He seemed to be always looking upwards when he was talking to people. Some very cruel people, including some children, teased Zacchaeus dreadfully, calling him names like 'Titch' and 'Shorty'. Sometimes, when they thought they were being really funny, they'd call him 'Lofty' which was worse!

Of course, people sometimes tease other people whom they like – they may even call them the same names – but they do it differently. Yet the way people spoke to Zacchaeus, he knew that they didn't like him one little bit. The trouble was that everybody thought he was a cheat. He might have been, but there again he might not. People aren't always right. The real trouble was that he was a tax collector. It was his job to see that people paid their taxes. And nobody likes someone who does that! So people said that he charged more than he should and kept the extra for himself. It might have been untrue, but nobody cared, because they liked getting at Zacchaeus. They didn't realise how unhappy that made him.

One day Zacchaeus heard that Jesus was coming to the town where he lived. How he would love to see Jesus! He'd never met him, but he'd heard that Jesus loved everybody.

'I wonder if he would even love me?' he thought. 'He'd be the first one!' So he washed, trimmed his beard, and went to look out for Jesus.

The trouble was that there were lots of crowds, and because Zacchaeus was small he couldn't see. So he climbed a tree to get a better view. Of course, the crowd loved it.

• They *pointed* up at him
• They *shook their fists*
• They *made horrible faces*

You can imagine them shouting nasty things like, 'Look at Zacchaeus, up a tree – now that's where he ought to live!' But when Jesus arrived they forgot about Zacchaeus.

Jesus saw Zacchaeus in the tree, and called out to him, 'What are you doing there?'

'Looking for you,' said Zacchaeus.

'Well, you won't find me up there,' said Jesus. 'Get down and go home – I'm having dinner with you.'

'What, me?' said Zacchaeus. 'Why do you want to visit me?'

'Well, not to pay my taxes,' said Jesus, 'they're up to date! Look Zacchaeus, does there have to be a reason?'

'I suppose not,' replied Zacchaeus.

'Good!' said Jesus. 'Because my feet ache, my eyes hurt from the sun, and my stomach's shouting out for food. So come down and let's go and eat.'

People couldn't understand why Jesus was going to have dinner with Zacchaeus. Sharing food with someone usually meant that they were a special friend. And everyone thought that being a good person was more important than anything else. They also thought that you could catch naughtiness, rather like a disease. For all those reasons, people who thought they were good didn't eat with people they thought were bad! So some people were angry with Jesus. 'He shouldn't go in there,' they said, 'Zacchaeus is a bad man!'

Zacchaeus was as amazed as everyone else! 'Who'd have thought,' he wondered, 'that Jesus would come to dinner with me!' Then he thought that if Jesus could like him that much then others might as well. He wasn't really so bad, after all! So he stood up and made a speech.

'I'm giving half of everything I have to charity,' he said. 'Wow!' thought all the people (who had followed to watch what happened). But that wasn't all.

'If I've cheated anyone,' Zacchaeus went on, 'I'll give them back four times as much!' Some of the people watching wondered whether they could pretend he'd cheated them, even though he hadn't.

But from then on, Zacchaeus became a kinder, happier man, and everyone wanted to go and have dinner with him!

Our Story

Tell the children about the preparation. Use one or two of the stories which were written or told. What do they think of the response of 'Spectator'?

Prayers

We're Glad

Jesus, you know us.
You know what is good
and what is bad in us
and you love us just the same.
Thank you.

We're Sad

Sometimes we love other people,
but sometimes we don't.
Sometimes, we're kind to people,
but sometimes we're not.
Sometimes, we say people are bad,
when we don't really know.
We're sorry.
Help us to see that everybody
has something good about them.
And forgive us, when we're unkind.

Let's Pray for People

Jesus, we know that some people are unhappy
because others are unkind to them.
Teach us all to be like you,
and to love all people,
whether we think they deserve it,
or whether we think they don't.
Then, perhaps, we might find out
good things about them.
Jesus, make us like you.

Songs

Jesus had all kinds of friends

– from *Wake up, World!*

Morning has broken
God knows me
One more step along the world I go

– from *Come and Praise*

Stand up! Walk tall!
Thank you, O God, for all our friends

– see *Appendix*

Jesus and the Tax Man

God's Story

Narrator   Zacchaeus was a small man – the kind who can easily get lost in a crowd. Some very cruel people, including some children, teased Zacchaeus dreadfully, calling him names like 'Titch' and 'Shorty'. Sometimes, when they thought they were being really funny, they'd call him 'Lofty' which was worse!

The way people spoke to Zacchaeus, he knew that they didn't like him one little bit.

Spectator   Zacchaeus is a cheat.

Narrator   Well you don't know that, do you? He might be, but there again he might not.

Spectator   Well, he's a tax collector, and nobody likes them!

Narrator   That's true. So people said that he was dishonest. They didn't realise how unhappy that made him.

Spectator   Didn't care much, either.

Narrator   One day Zacchaeus heard that Jesus was coming to his town. He'd never met him, but he'd heard the Jesus loved everybody.

Zacchaeus   I wonder if he would even be nice to someone like me?

Spectator   He'd be the first one if he did!

Narrator   Zacchaeus washed, trimmed his beard, and went to look out for Jesus. The trouble was that there were lots of crowds, and little Zacchaeus couldn't see. So he climbed a tree to get a better view.

- They *pointed* up at him
- They *shook their fists*
- They *made horrible faces!*

Spectator Look at Zacchaeus, up a tree – now that's where he ought to live! Hey, Lofty – Have a banana?

Narrator When Jesus saw Zacchaeus, he was kinder to him.

Jesus What are you doing there, Zacchaeus?

Zacchaeus Looking for you.

Jesus Well, you won't find me up there! Get down and go home – I'm having dinner with you.

Zacchaeus What, me? Why do you want to visit me?

Jesus Well, not to pay my taxes – they're up to date! Look Zacchaeus, does there have to be a reason?

Zacchaeus I suppose not.

Jesus Good! Because my feet ache, my eyes hurt from the sun, and my stomach's shouting out for food. So come down and let's go and eat.

Narrator People couldn't understand why Jesus was going to have dinner with Zacchaeus. Sharing food with someone usually meant that they were a special friend. And people who thought they were good didn't eat with people they thought were bad! So some people were angry with Jesus.

Spectator He shouldn't go in there; Zacchaeus is a bad man! I'm going along to watch and see what happens.

Narrator Zacchaeus was as amazed as everyone else! So he stood up and made a speech.

Zacchaeus I'm giving half of everything I have to charity, and if I've cheated anyone I'll give them back four times as much!

Spectator Wow! That's a turn up – I wonder if he'll believe me if I pretend he's cheated me.

Narrator From then on, Zacchaeus became a kinder, happier man, and everyone wanted to go and have dinner with him!

The Donkey's Day Out

Based on Luke 19:29-40

BEFORE THE DAY

Talk with the children about kings and queens, emperors etc. What do the children associate with them? Get them to draw pictures. Perhaps they could make some simple costumes (cardboard crowns etc.) and dress up as rulers.

• Think about the actions for all the children to join in during the story.

ON THE DAY

Introduction

Today we have a bible story told by a very special somebody; somebody who can be very stubborn and hard to budge. But he carries away the best prize of all. First we'll say our 'Thank you' prayer.

'Thank you' Prayer

Thank you, God, for all you give us,
thank you for the earth and sea;
thank you, God, for special people,
thank you, God, for making me.

God's Story

Well, there I was, munching on a mouthful of hay – because that's what donkeys do – when along came these two men and started to untie me from the wall. I suppose some donkeys would have been pleased – freedom and all that – but I knew there must be work for me to do, and as it was a hot day, and the hay was tasty, I wasn't very keen. Besides, my mother always told me not to go off with strangers. So I just dug my hooves in and refused to budge! You should have seen them trying to move me!

• They *pulled me from in front*
• They *pushed me from behind*
• They *got cross* and *waved their arms about*

And they used some words which well brought up religious people shouldn't even have known about! Then, just as it was getting really interesting, my owner came out and spoilt it.

'Hey!' he shouted, 'What do you think you're doing with my donkey?'

One of the men said, 'The master needs it,' and to my amazement, my owner just said, 'All right,' and told me to stop mucking about.

I nearly said, 'Mucking about? You ain't seen nothing yet!' but I remembered some advice my mum gave me. 'Never talk to humans,' she'd said, 'It upsets them – they like to think they're the only ones who can do it.' So, off we went, and I had the time of my life!

When we got near Jerusalem, we met up with Jesus and his friends. Jesus sat on my back, and we set off into the town. What a racket! People were singing, dancing and spreading their clothes on the road for me to walk on. Don't you do that sort of thing, though or you won't half get into trouble. Human parents are really fussy about clothes!

I was getting a bit worried in case there was trouble. Some of the important leaders came over and said to Jesus, 'Can't you shut this rabble up?'

But Jesus laughed, 'Shut them up?' he said. 'Impossible! There's so much joy around today that if the people didn't shout, the stones probably would!'

That told them!

Mind you, it was a bit scary. I thought for a minute that Jesus was actually going to try to take over, and revolutions aren't really my thing. But he just went to the temple and caused a bit of a scene, while I was tied up outside. It turned out that Jesus didn't like the traders selling things in the temple, and so he threw them out – jolly good thing too!

Afterwards two more of Jesus' friends, Philip and Andrew, took me home. On the way, Philip said, 'It's strange – why didn't he ride a horse, like a real king – instead of this scruffy donkey.' (I tell you, I nearly refused to go another step! 'Scruffy donkey,' indeed! But my mum always said, 'Never cut off your nose to spite your face,' so as we were going home, and I was tired, I pretended I hadn't heard.)

Andrew explained, 'Jesus doesn't want to be the kind of king everyone's afraid of. He loves the people and he wants them to love him. So he didn't want anything impressive – just an ordinary mule.' It got worse! 'Ordinary'! and 'Mule'! I bet I've got a better pedigree than either of those two fellows had! They will never know how close they came to being in real trouble. But we were nearly home, so I just kept on going.

I liked Jesus – he seemed different. And he treated me well. Yes, I like Jesus. But his friends – oh dear! I'm afraid they've got an awful lot to learn!

Our Story

Use the prepared material to talk about 'majesty'. What would the children think if the queen came to their school riding a bicycle? If you have someone dressed up, let them 'play the queen/king' for a few minutes. Then speak about Jesus' idea of kingship expressed in the story.

Prayers

We're Glad

Thank you Jesus,
for loving us,
and wanting us to love you.
Thank you for being kind to us,
and for not bossing us around!

We're Sad

We're not always kind to other people.
Sometimes we like to be bossy
when we don't need to be;
we want people to think we are good,
and we end up by hurting them –
and making ourselves look silly,
at the same time.
We're sorry.
Help us to love people more.

Let's Pray for People

We know that some people have to give orders, and everyone has to take them from somebody. We pray for people who tell others what to do:
help them to be kind,
to show respect,
to love, and to be loved.

Songs

Keep on travelling on!
Out to the great wide world we go!
Pick up your feet and go!

– from *Wake up, World!*

One more step along the world I go
Kum ba yah

– from *Come and Praise*

Stand up! Walk tall!

– see *Appendix*

The Donkey's Day Out

God's Story

Donkey   Well, there I was, munching on a mouthful of hay – because that's what donkeys do – when along came these two men and started to untie me from the wall. I suppose some donkeys would have been pleased but I wasn't very keen. Besides, my mother always told me not to go off with strangers. So I just dug my hooves in and refused to budge! You should have seen them trying to move me!

- They *pulled me from in front*
- They *pushed me from behind*
- They *got cross* and *waved their arms about*

And they used some words which well brought up religious people shouldn't even have known about! Then, just as it was getting really interesting, my owner came out and spoilt it.

Owner   Hey! What do you think you're doing with my donkey?

Thomas   The master needs it.

Owner   All right. Now you stop mucking about, and go with these people!

Donkey   'Mucking about' indeed! I nearly said, 'You ain't seen nothing yet!' But I remembered some advice my mum gave me. 'Never talk to humans,' she'd said. 'It upsets them – they like to think they're the only ones who can do it.' So, off we went, and I had the time of my life!

When we got near Jerusalem, we met up with Jesus and his friends. Jesus sat on my back, and we set off into the town. What a racket! People were singing, dancing and spreading their clothes on the road for me to walk on.

I was getting a bit worried in case there was trouble. Some of the important leaders came over and gave Thomas a message for Jesus.

Thomas   Er, Jesus, some of the lawyers have asked if you can shut the people up.

Jesus   Shut them up? Impossible! There's so much joy around today that if the people didn't shout, the stones probably would!

Donkey   That told them! Mind you, it was a bit scary. I thought for a minute that Jesus was actually going to try to take over, and revolutions aren't really my thing. But he just went to the temple and caused a bit of a scene, while I was tied up outside. It turned out that Jesus didn't like the traders selling things in the temple, and so he threw them out – jolly good thing too! Then Thomas and Andrew took me home. I didn't think much of their conversation!

Thomas   It's strange – why didn't he ride a horse, like a real king – instead of this scruffy donkey?

Donkey   I tell you, I nearly refused to go another step! 'Scruffy donkey,' indeed! But my mum always said, 'Never cut off your nose to spite your face,' so as we were going home, and I was tired, I pretended I hadn't heard.

Andrew   Jesus doesn't want to be the kind of king everyone's afraid of. He loves the people and he wants them to love him. So he didn't want anything impressive – just an ordinary mule.

Donkey   It got worse! 'Ordinary'! and 'Mule'! I bet I've got a better pedigree than either of those two fellows had! They will never know how close they came to being in real trouble. But we were nearly home, so I just kept on going.

    I liked Jesus – he seemed different. And he treated me well. Yes, I like Jesus. But his friends – oh dear! I'm afraid they've got an awful lot to learn!

A Stranger On The Road

Based on Luke 24:13-35

BEFORE THE DAY

What do the children do when they're unhappy? Do they go to a special person, or place? Perhaps their bedroom provides a retreat, or maybe they have a special toy which serves as a 'security blanket'. You could make a list (probably without names on it) or get the children to draw, or just prepare a short talk on the basis of what you have done.

• Think about the actions for all the children to join in during the story.

ON THE DAY
Introduction

This story is about a wonderful surprise that happened to two sad people when they least expected it. But first we'll say our 'Thank you' prayer.

'Thank you' Prayer

Thank you, God, for all you give us,
thank you for the earth and sea;
thank you, God, for special people,
thank you, God, for making me.

God's Story

Cleopas and his wife Joanna lived in a village called Emmaus, about seven miles from Jerusalem. They had gone to Jerusalem for a big festival, and to see Jesus. But when they got there, they heard that Jesus had been captured by some bad people, and had been killed. What they didn't know was that God had brought Jesus back to life.

'Let's go home,' said Joanna, 'I don't like it here, any more.'

'Neither do I,' said Cleopas, 'the place is full of terrible memories.'

So they set out to walk the seven miles home. It was beginning to get dark when a stranger started to catch up with them. Joanna was saying, 'I can't understand how it happened. Jesus had so many friends, you'd have thought they'd have stopped it.'

'Stopped what?' asked the stranger, who had drawn level with them. 'What's happened?'

'You must have been walking around with your eyes closed!' said Cleopas. 'Jesus was killed – just because some powerful people were jealous of him.'

'Oh, that!' said the stranger. 'If you'd been reading your Bible, you'd have expected it. People like Jesus always get on the wrong side of powerful people.'

'We did hear a rumour that God had brought him back to life,' said Joanna.

'Yes,' said Cleopas impatiently, 'but that was just some silly women – we men knew it wasn't true!'

Cleopas and Joanna did not know that this stranger was Jesus himself! The 'silly women' had been right! But they didn't recognise him, and he walked with them talking about the bible, and how it said that God's special helper was going to get himself into trouble. By the time they got home to Emmaus, they were feeling better.

'It's a dreadful shame that Jesus was killed,' said Cleopas. 'But perhaps God's at work in all this somewhere.'

'Oh, yes, I think he is,' said the stranger mysteriously. 'God doesn't like bad things happening, but sometimes he can do amazing things with them!'

By this time, they were at the door of Cleopas' and Joanna's house. 'Boy, am I glad to be home!' exclaimed Joanna. 'Here we can feel safe. Nothing exciting happens here, and we always know where we stand.'

'Really?' said the stranger. 'I wouldn't bank on that, if I were you. Goodnight.' And he started to move on.

'Just a minute,' called Cleopas. 'It's late. Please come and stay with us.'

'Thank you,' said the stranger, and followed them in to the house. They soon had a warm fire going, and put some bread on the table. Just as Cleopas was about to offer the food round, the stranger did a very odd thing. Instead of being waited on by Cleopas and Joanna, like a guest, *he served them!*

- He *picked up* the bread
- He *broke it* into pieces
- He *handed it round*

'That's strange,' thought Cleopas, 'he's our guest, but he's serving us.'

'Good heavens!' Joanna exclaimed suddenly. 'It's Jesus!'

'So it is!' cried Cleopas, joyfully, and they both went to hug Jesus at the same time. But he wasn't there! He'd gone!

'Come on!' said Cleopas. 'We've got to get back.' They scurried back to Jerusalem and burst into the room where Jesus' other friends were.

'Guess what!' panted Joanna.

'No,' said Philip, 'you guess what! Jesus is alive again – it's true. We know it's true, because Simon told us.'

Joanna nearly said, 'Oh, so you believe a man, do you?' but she didn't want to spoil the evening. Everyone was wonderfully happy. They kept on telling the stories to each other of how they had found out.

'Just think,' said Cleopas to Joanna, 'a few hours ago, Jerusalem was a terrible place, and now it's the best!'

'Yes,' said Joanna. 'That often seems to happen when Jesus is around.'

Our Story

Talk about retreats. Use the display if you have one; otherwise tell the whole group about the kinds of things your group discussed. This story shows us that, when we need to get away, Jesus understands. He doesn't try to stop us, or turn us back, but he goes with us and gives us the confidence to go back when we are ready.

Prayers

We're Glad

Thank you, Jesus,
for being our friend.
Thank you for always being with us,
wherever we are,
and whatever we're doing.
Thank you for never leaving us
to cope on our own.

We're Sad

Sometimes, we run away,
just when people need us.
We don't want to face up to things,
or do difficult jobs.
We're sorry, Jesus,
help us to be brave.

Let's Pray for People

Please, God, help people who are frightened,
and who want to run away.
Help them to know that you're still there,
still caring.
And if they can't recognise you,
because they're confused or unhappy,
show us the best way to help them

Songs

You can't pin Jesus down!
Pick up your feet and go!
I'm black, I'm white, I'm short, I'm tall
In the winter, nights are dark

– from *Wake up, World!*

Thank you, O God, for all our friends

– see *Appendix*

A Stranger On The Road

God's Story

Narrator   Cleopas and Joanna lived in a village called Emmaus, about seven miles from Jerusalem. They had gone to Jerusalem for a big festival, and to see Jesus. But Jesus had been captured by some bad people, and had been killed.

Joanna   Let's go home! I don't like it here any more.

Cleopas   Neither do I; the place is full of terrible memories.

Narrator   So they set out to walk the seven miles home. It was beginning to get dark when a stranger caught up with them, and heard what Joanna was saying.

Joanna   I can't understand how it happened. Jesus had so many friends, you'd have thought they'd have stopped it.

Stranger   Stopped what? What's happened?

Cleopas   You must have been walking around with your eyes closed! Jesus was killed – just because some powerful people were jealous of him.

Stranger   Oh, that! If you'd been reading your Bible, you'd have expected it. People like Jesus always get on the wrong side of powerful people.

Joanna   We did hear a rumour that God had brought him back to life.

Cleopas   Yes, but that was just some silly women – we men knew it wasn't true!

Narrator   Cleopas and Joanna did not know that this stranger was Jesus himself! The 'silly women' had been right! He walked with them talking how the Bible said that God's special helper was going to get himself into trouble. By the time they got home, they were feeling better.

Cleopas   It's a dreadful shame that Jesus was killed, but perhaps God's at work in all this somewhere.

Stranger   Oh, yes, I think he is. God doesn't like bad things happening, but sometimes he can do amazing things with them when they do!

Joanna   Well, this is our house. Boy, am I glad to be home! Here we can feel safe. Nothing exciting happens here.

Stranger   Really? I wouldn't bank on that, if I were you. Goodnight.

Cleopas   Just a minute. It's late. Please come and stay with us.

Stranger   Thank you.

Narrator   The stranger followed them in to the house. They soon had a warm fire going, and put some bread on the table. Then the stranger did a very odd thing. Instead of being waited on like a guest, *he served them!*

- He *picked up* the bread
- He *broke it* into pieces
- He *handed it round*

Joanna   Good heavens! It's Jesus!

Cleopas   So it is!

Narrator   They both went to hug Jesus. But he wasn't there!

Cleopas   Come on! We've got to get back.

Narrator   They scurried back to Jerusalem to tell their story. Philip said they already knew Jesus was alive because Simon had told them so. Everyone was wonderfully happy, and kept on telling the stories to each other.

Cleopas   Just think: a few hours ago, Jerusalem was a terrible place, and now it's the best!

Joanna   Yes. That often seems to happen when Jesus is around.

A Wedding with no Wine

Based on John 2:1-11

BEFORE THE DAY

Think about fun, about celebrations, about parties. What do the children really enjoy doing? Perhaps they could either draw some pictures or bring in some objects which represent their interests, such as games, books etc., to form a display.

• Think about the actions for all the children to join in during the story.

ON THE DAY

Introduction

We're going to hear a story about Jesus helping some people to enjoy themselves. But first we'll say our 'Thank you' prayer.

'Thank you' Prayer

Thank you, God, for all you give us,
thank you for the earth and sea;
thank you, God, for special people,
thank you, God, for making me.

God's Story

Jake and Sarah were a lovely couple who lived not far from Nazareth, where Jesus lived. They had been saving their money for a long time, because they were getting married. They'd invited lots of friends, including Jesus and his mother. When the big day came all the neighbourhood turned out to see the couple pass on their way to the wedding, and quite a lot of them actually went to the ceremony. Jake and Sarah promised to love each other for the rest of their lives, and everybody cheered. Then they went to the reception. Of course, the usual speeches were made, and the usual toast was drunk:

• They *raised their glasses*
• They *shouted 'To life!'*
• They *drank their wine*

The caterer was getting worried. 'They're drinking a lot more than I expected,' he said, 'and I think the wine's going to run out.'

He'd hardly said it when his head waiter came up and said, 'We've run out of wine. And if you don't do something about it, we'll never be asked to do another wedding within a hundred miles of here!'

Mary, Jesus' mother, noticed and asked Jesus to help. At first, Jesus wasn't very keen, but Mary knew that he wouldn't let people go thirsty. So she went over to the caterer and said, 'My son's over there – second from the end of the third table – he'll help.'

The caterer went over to Jesus, and said, 'Er, I'm afraid this is rather embarrassing, sir, but . . .'

'I bet it is,' smiled Jesus, 'you're out of wine, aren't you? You'll have to use those big jugs of water by the door.'

In those days, people got very dusty from walking, and whenever someone visited you you would give them water to wash their feet. It was good manners. And that was what the jars of water were for. The caterer was horrified.

'You can't use that!' he said. 'It's not even drinking water – it's straight from the river!'

'Trust him,' said Mary, 'and do whatever he says.'

So two waiters brought the jars to Jesus. The jars were very heavy! 'Now what do we do?' gasped one of the waiters.

'Pour some out,' said Jesus, 'and let the bridegroom taste it.'

The waiter thought Jesus was potty, but his boss just nodded at him. So they poured out a glassful and took it to Jake. The waiter hurried out to help with the washing up – anything was better than being around when Jake tasted the dirty water! Sure enough, he heard Jake shouting, 'Where's the caterer? Someone find me the caterer!'

'Oh dear,' thought the waiter, 'now we're for it, but he did tell me to do it.'

The caterer went over to Jake, intending to blame the waiter for making a mistake. But Jake was very pleased! 'Most caterers use the worst wine at the end,' he exclaimed, 'because they think the guests will be too drunk to notice. But you've saved the best!'

'Oh! Er – well – um – all part of the service, sir!' said the astonished caterer, and hurried over to Jesus. 'I don't know who you are,' he said, 'but you've saved me some embarrassment today, all right!'

Jesus smiled and said, 'I'm glad you're happy.'

The word soon got around, and everyone was talking about Jesus. 'I can't understand it!' people would say. 'He's obviously a holy man, but he really wants everyone to be happy.' Whenever Jesus heard people say it, he would answer that there's nothing strange in that. 'God wants everyone to be happy,' he would say. 'He just doesn't want you to make other people unhappy in the process.'

Now there's really nothing strange about that, is there?

Our Story

Draw attention to the display. Point out that God likes to see us enjoying life – just as long as we aren't doing it selfishly. God's got nothing against fun!

Prayers

We're Glad

Thank you, Jesus,
for wanting us to be happy.
Thank you for sharing life with us,
and for being there
when things go wrong.

We're Sad

Sometimes we're unhappy,
because we can't have
everything we want.
We get grumpy,
and we forget all the good things
we already have.
Then we upset others.
We're sorry.
Help us to be happy
with what we've got.

Let's Pray for People

Jesus, our friend,
we know you want us to be happy,
but some people are very sad.
They think you don't approve of fun,
or laugh at jokes.
They think they shouldn't enjoy life.
So they make themselves unhappy,
and other people as well.
We pray for them:
help them to be happy,
and not to feel guilty.
Tell them that you love life,
and want them to enjoy it, too!

Songs

Jesus turned the water into wine
God made the earth
I'm black, I'm white, I'm short, I'm tall
Out to the great wide world we go

– from *Wake up, World!*

Morning has broken
All things bright and beautiful

– from *Come and Praise*

Come and celebrate

– from *Songs of Fellowship*

A Wedding with no Wine

God's Story

Narrator Jake and Sarah were a lovely couple who lived not far from Nazareth, where Jesus lived. They had been saving their money for a long time, because they were getting married. They'd invited lots of friends, including Jesus and his mother. When the big day came, all the neighbourhood turned out to see the couple pass on their way to the wedding, and quite a lot of them actually went to the ceremony. Jake and Sarah promised to love each other for the rest of their lives, and everybody cheered. Then they went to the reception. Of course, the usual speeches were made, and the usual toast was drunk.

- They *raised their glasses*
- They *shouted 'To life!'*
- They *drank their wine*

Narrator The caterer was getting worried.

Caterer They're drinking a lot more than I expected and I think the wine's going to run out. If that happens, I'll never be asked to do another wedding within a hundred miles of here!

Narrator Mary knew that Jesus wouldn't let people go thirsty. So she went over to speak to the caterer.

Mary My son's over there – second from the end of the third table – he'll help.

Narrator So the caterer went over to Jesus.

Caterer Er, I'm afraid this is rather embarrassing, sir, but . . .

Jesus I bet it is! You're out of wine, aren't you? You'll have to use those big jugs of water by the door.

Caterer   You can't use that – it's for washing in! It's not even drinking water – it's straight from the river!

Mary   Trust him and do whatever he says.

Narrator   So the caterer had the jars brought to Jesus. The jars were very heavy!

Caterer   Now what do we do?

Jesus   Pour some out, and let Jake taste it.

Narrator   So they poured out a glassful and took it to Jake.

Jake   Where's the caterer? Someone find me the caterer!

Caterer   Here I am, sir. I'm dreadfully sorry – I think one of the waiters must have made a mistake.

Jake   Mistake? I don't think so – this wine's terrific! Most caterers use the worst wine at the end, because they think the guests will be too drunk to notice. But you've saved the best!

Caterer   Oh! Er – well – um – all part of the service, sir!
(Turns to Jesus)
I don't know who you are, but you've saved me some embarrassment today, all right!

Jesus   I'm glad you're happy.

Caterer   It's strange – I know you're quite a religious person, but you still want everyone to be really happy.

Jesus   There's nothing strange in that. God wants everyone to be happy. He just doesn't want them to make other people unhappy, in the process. Now there's really nothing strange about that, is there?

Well, Well, Well!

Based on John 4:5-42

BEFORE THE DAY

How many different kinds of people are there? Get the children to draw pictures of different kinds of people – different colours of skin, different colours/styles of hair and so on. Should we be afraid of people, just because they're different? Could a special speaker be invited to the assembly from the local Council of Faiths or Race Relations Council?

• Think about the actions for all the children to join in during the story.

ON THE DAY

Introduction

Sometimes we don't like people for silly reasons: just because they come from a different place, or perhaps because they speak differently from us. We're going to hear a story about how Jesus dealt with that sort of prejudice, in a moment , but first we'll say our 'Thank you' prayer.

'Thank you' Prayer

Thank you, God, for all you give us,
thank you for the earth and sea;
thank you, God, for special people,
thank you, God, for making me.

God's Story

Jesus and his friends were out for a walk. 'I don't know why he's brought us this way,' grumbled Thomas. 'It's really a very rough area.'

'You're right,' said Philip. 'The people can't be trusted.'

'There's a very high crime rate here, you know,' added Matthew.

Jesus just kept on walking, until they came to a well. Then he said, 'This is a good place – let's have a picnic. There are some shops not far away; why don't you go and buy some food?'

'What – go in there?' said Thomas. 'Not on my own.'

'I meant all of you,' said Jesus. 'I'll be all right here.'

Jesus' friends weren't at all sure about that. 'We can't leave him here on his own,' said Matthew. 'You know what Jesus is like – he'll talk to anybody – and round here that's not a good idea.'

'That's true,' said Judas. 'He's so soft, he tries to be friends with some very doubtful people.'

'You mean', Peter interrupted, 'people like swindlers and thieves?' Matthew and Judas blushed, and Peter said, 'Come on, Jesus can look after himself.'

So the disciples went away, while Jesus sat down at the well. Just as he was thinking how thirsty he was, a woman came up with a cup in one hand and a bucket in the other to get some water. 'I wonder if you could give me a drink from your cup?' asked Jesus. The woman, whose name was Becky, was suspicious.

'You're not from these parts, are you?' she asked. 'You're from the other side of the hill. People like you don't talk to people like me – we're different. You go to one kind of church and I go to another. If your friends knew you were talking to me – let alone asking me for a favour – they'd be very cross with you.'

'But all I'm asking for is a cup of water,' said Jesus. 'I can give you something much more exciting than that. I could change your life. Why don't you go and get your husband, so that I can tell him, too.'

'I haven't got a husband,' she answered.

'Not at the moment,' said Jesus. 'But you've had quite a few, haven't you? Tell you what, go and get the friends you're living with.'

'How on earth did you know about that?' asked Becky, but before Jesus could reply the disciples came trudging back with the food they had bought.

'There!' said Matthew, 'I knew this would happen – he's got talking to one of those dreadful women from the neighbourhood.'

- Matthew *pointed his finger at the woman*
- He *spread his hands*
- He *turned his back on her*

'Oh, don't be such a snob,' said Peter. 'None of us is perfect. Anyway, Jesus seems to have survived. She's just a woman like any other – people haven't got two heads around here, you know.'

As the disciples got closer, Becky said to Jesus, 'I'd better go, before your friends give you a hard time. I'll go and tell my village about you!'

So off she went, back to her neighbours and her family. 'I've just met the most amazing man,' she said, 'from the other side of the hill.'

Her neighbours were horrified. 'From the other side of the hill?' they asked. 'Surely you didn't talk to him – you can't trust those people, you know.'

'That's funny,' said Becky. 'That's what his friends were saying about us. But he's really worth meeting. He knew all about me.'

Eventually Becky's sister Judy agreed to go back with her – and all the neighbours went as well to keep an eye on them! When they met Jesus, they were amazed. It finished up with everyone talking to each other, and they all forgot completely about which side of the hill everybody came from!

Well, well, well!

Our Story

Draw attention to the display, and/or introduce the special speaker. Show how, when we understand people better, the mere fact that they are different need not in itself make us afraid of them.

Prayers

We're Glad

We're glad, Jesus,
that people aren't all the same.
Thank you for showing us
how to love one another,
and not be afraid.

We're Sad

Jesus, we're sorry for being unkind
to people who are different from us.
They may believe different things
go to different kinds of churches,
like different kinds of food,
and have different ideas about life,
but you love them all.
Help us to love them too,
and help us to see that, to them,
it's we who are peculiar!

Let's Pray for People

We pray for all people who are lonely
or who are angry
because of the way other people treat them.
We pray for people who are afraid of others
just because they're different.
We pray for ourselves.

Songs

I'm black, I'm white, I'm short, I'm tall
Jesus had all kinds of friends
Out to the great wide world we go

– from *Wake up, World!*

Water of life
When I needed a neighbour

– from *Come and Praise*

Well, Well, Well!

– see *Appendix*

Well, Well, Well!

God's Story

Narrator   Jesus and his friends were out for a walk. Judas wasn't happy.

Judas   I don't know why he's brought us this way; it's really a very rough area. The people can't be trusted.

Narrator   The others were agreeing with Judas, but Jesus just kept on walking, until they came to a well.

Jesus   This is a good place for a picnic. There are some shops not far away. Why don't you go and buy some food?'

Narrator   Jesus' friends weren't too sure about that.

Judas   We can't leave him here on his own. You know what Jesus is like – he'll talk to anybody – he tries to be friends with some very doubtful people.

Peter   You mean, people like swindlers and thieves? Come on, Jesus can look after himself.

Narrator   So the disciples went away, while Jesus sat down at the well. A woman called Becky came up with a cup in one hand and a bucket in the other to get some water.

Jesus   I wonder if you could give me a drink from your cup?

Becky   You're from the other side of the hill. People like you don't talk to people like me – we're different. You go to one kind of church and I go to another. If your friends knew you were talking to me – let alone asking me for a favour – they'd be very cross with you.

Jesus   I could change your life, you know. Why don't you go and get your husband so that I can tell him, too?

Becky   I haven't got a husband.

Jesus	But you've had quite a few, haven't you? Tell you what, go and get the friends you're living with.
Becky	How on earth did you know about that?
Narrator	Before Jesus could reply, the disciples came trudging back with the food they had bought.
Matthew	There! I knew it. He's got talking to one of those dreadful women from the neighbourhood.
Narrator	How do you think Matthew showed his feelings?

- He *pointed his finger* at the woman
- He *shook his head sadly*
- He *turned his back* on her

Peter	Oh, don't be such a snob! None of us is perfect. Anyway, Jesus seems to have survived. She's just a woman like any other – people haven't got two heads around here, you know.
Becky	I'd better go, before your friends give you a hard time. I'll go and tell my friends about you!
Narrator	So off she went, and the first person she met was her neighbour, Judy.
Becky	I've just met the most amazing man, from the other side of the hill.
Judy	From the other side of the hill? Surely you didn't talk to him – you can't trust those people, you know.
Becky	That's funny; that's what his friends were saying about us. But he's really worth meeting.
Narrator	When the neighbours met Jesus, they were amazed. They all finished up talking to each other, and forgot completely about which side of the hill everybody came from! Well, well, well!

The Biggest Picnic in History

Based on John 6:1-14

BEFORE THE DAY

Ask the children to identify their favourite foods. Try to get a variety of things - sweet and savoury, fresh and processed. You could create a very interesting display, using food items, packets, wrappers, cooking utensils etc.

• Think about the actions for all the children to join in during the story.

ON THE DAY

Introduction

We're going to hear a story about a great big picnic shortly, but first we'll say our 'Thank you' prayer.

'Thank you' Prayer

Thank you, God, for all you give us,
thank you for the earth and sea;
thank you, God, for special people,
thank you, God, for making me.

God's Story

Sam was well known in his neighbourhood, with his uncombed curly hair, freckles and a big, permanent grin. He also loved listening to stories. It didn't really matter what they were about – he just enjoyed listening to them. So of course when he heard that Jesus was in the area, he wanted to go and listen. No-one could tell a story quite the way Jesus did – they were all about the kind of people and places everyone knew well; and the way he told them, you just couldn't help listening. So Sam was really excited.

'Mum! Mum! Jesus is here! Can I go and listen to him?'

Well, Mum knew that she wouldn't get any peace until she said 'Yes', but she didn't let Sam go just like that. 'Take some food with you,' she said. 'Once you start listening to that Jesus fellow, you're likely to be there all day!' She was right. Once Sam got listening to a good story, he'd forget about everything – including going home for tea!

Jesus wasn't actually planning on telling any stories that day; he really wanted to rest. So he took his disciples away into the hills, and didn't tell anybody where they were going. Unfortunately, it was about as hard to keep a secret, where Jesus lived as it is in X[1], so it wasn't long before just about everyone knew where Jesus was! And before long, the 'quiet place' was full of people – about five thousand of them! 'Well,' said Jesus, 'that's our peace and quiet done for!'

Jesus spent a lot of time talking to people, and as time went by he knew that they would be hungry – he always remembered about what people needed, even when they forgot about it themselves! So he said to Philip, 'Can we buy these people any food?'

'We can't afford all that!' said Philip.

Sam thought he'd better try to help – so he went to see Andrew, another of Jesus' friends. 'Look,' he said. 'I've got five bread rolls, and a couple of fish.'

Andrew didn't think that would be very helpful, but he didn't want to be unkind. 'Let's see what Jesus says,' he suggested.

'Well,' said Jesus, 'I think we can do something with this. Tell everyone to sit down, and we'll share out the food we have.'

Jesus' friends didn't think there would be enough, but they knew that Jesus usually turned out to be right. 'Come on,' said Andrew, 'let's do it. James, you start over there, and John go to that side.'

So the people sat down and shared the food.

• They *broke up the bread*
• They *shared it out*
• They *ate* as much as they needed

And can you guess what happened? Everyone had enough to eat! Not only that – when they picked up all the bits that had been dropped, they had another twelve baskets full of food.

Everyone thought Jesus was just the person

they'd been waiting for. 'He ought to be our king,' they said. 'He'd be a lot better than Herod.'

Jesus didn't want that at all. Palaces, fancy clothes and servants bowing and scraping weren't his cup of tea! So he turned to his friends, and said, 'I think it's time to find that quiet place we were looking for!' And as Jesus and his friends slipped away, Sam went home.

'Well?' asked Mum, when he got back, 'What stories did Jesus tell today?'

'Oh,' said Sam, 'he told a few good ones, but what was really exciting was what Jesus *did*!'

Don't you agree?

Our Story

Draw attention to the display, and get the children talking about their favourite foods. How would they feel if they couldn't get them – or even their second favourite? Is it fair that we can pick and choose while others can't even get the basic necessities? Are there ways we can help?

Prayers

We're Glad

Thank you, God,
for our food.
We like lots of different things,
and we know that they all come
from you.
Thank you for our food.

We're Sad

Sometimes, we're greedy.
We eat more than we need.
Other times, we throw food away;
we waste it.
We know some people are hungry,
and we could help them
more than we do.
We're sorry.

Let's Pray for People

Jesus, give us the things we need,
and help us not to be greedy,
or wasteful.
Bless all the people who grow our food
or pack it
or bring it to us,
and help us to care for others
who don't have enough.

Songs

Feed the hungry people
God made the earth

– from *Wake up, World!*

God knows me
When I needed a neighbour
Kum ba yah

– from *Come and Praise*

Thank you, O God, for all our friends

– see *Appendix*

The Biggest Picnic in History

God's Story

Narrator   Sam was well-known in his neighbourhood, with his uncombed curly hair, freckles and a big, permanent grin. He also loved listening to stories. It didn't really matter what they were about – he just enjoyed listening to them. So of course when he heard that Jesus was in the area, he wanted to go and listen. No-one could tell a story quite the way Jesus did – they were all about the kind of people and places everyone knew well; and the way he told them, you just couldn't help listening. So Sam was really excited.

Sam   Mum! Mum! Jesus is here! Can I go and listen to him?

Mum   Well, I suppose I'll get no peace if I say 'no'! But you'd better take some food with you - once you start listening to that Jesus fellow, you're likely to be there all day!

Narrator   She was right. Once Sam got listening to a good story, he'd forget about everything – including going home for tea! Now Jesus wasn't actually planning on telling any stories that day; he really wanted to rest. So he took his disciples away into the hills, and didn't tell anybody where they were going. Unfortunately, it was about as hard to keep a secret, where Jesus lived as it is in - - - - - - - - - - - - - -[2], so it wasn't long before just about everyone knew where Jesus was! And before long, the 'quiet place' was full of people – about five thousand of them!

Jesus   Well, that's our peace and quiet done for! But these people must be hungry. Andrew, can we buy them any food?

Andrew   We can't afford all that!

Narrator   Sam thought he'd better try to help – so he went to see Andrew.

---

[2] The name of your town or village

Sam   Look, I've got five bread rolls, and a couple of fish.

Andrew   Hmm . . . Well, let's see what Jesus says.

Jesus   I think we can do something with this. Tell everyone to sit down, and we'll share out the food we have.

Andrew   It doesn't look very hopeful to me, but if you say so, Jesus, we'll give it a go. James, you start over there, and John go to that side.

Narrator   So the people sat down, and shared the food.

- They *broke up the bread*
- They *shared it out*
- They *ate* as much as they needed

And can you guess what happened? Everyone had enough to eat! Not only that – when they picked up all the bits that had been dropped, they had another twelve baskets full of food. Everyone thought Jesus was just the person they'd been waiting for. They wanted to make him king – after all, he'd be a lot better than Herod! But Jesus didn't want that at all. Palaces, fancy clothes and servants bowing and scraping weren't his cup of tea!

Jesus   I think it's time to find that quiet place we were looking for – before things get out of hand.

Narrator   As Jesus and his friends slipped away, Sam went home to Mum.

Mum   Well? What stories did Jesus tell today?

Sam   Oh, he told a few good ones, but what was really exciting was what Jesus *did*!

Narrator   Don't you agree?

Living in Glass Houses

Based on John 8:3-11

BEFORE THE DAY

Ask the children to write down something good – and nothing bad! – about every other person in the class (without using individual names). For each child, there is bound to be at least one other who presents difficulty in this respect! You can then pin the pieces of paper onto a board for display, perhaps with some self-portraits drawn by the children!

• Think about the actions for all the children to join in during the story.

ON THE DAY

Introduction

I expect you've heard it said that, 'People who live in glass houses shouldn't throw stones'? We're going to hear a story a bit like that in a few minutes, but first we'll say our 'Thank you' prayer.

'Thank you' Prayer

Thank you, God, for all you give us,
thank you for the earth and sea;
thank you, God, for special people,
thank you, God, for making me.

God's Story

One day, Jesus and his friends heard a dreadful noise. Everyone turned to see what it was. Then, out of one of the side streets came a large crowd, dragging a woman along. She was screaming and shouting, begging them to let her go. Jesus was horrified.

'We've got to stop this,' he said. 'Look what they're doing to that poor woman.'

His friends weren't so sure. 'I'd be careful, if I were you,' said Matthew. 'There may be a good reason for it.'

'There's never a good reason to treat anyone like that!' replied Jesus. 'Whatever she's done, she's a human being.'

'Well,' said James, 'I'd keep out of it. It's always best not to get involved.'

Jesus wasn't at all pleased by that, and was going to say something very stern to James, but by that time the crowd were almost on top of them. They were really wound up!

• They were *rolling up their sleeves*
• They were *picking up stones*
• They were *taking aim*

'What on earth do you think you are doing?' Jesus asked the leader of the mob. The man, a nasty, vindictive character called Josh, said, 'We're going to kill her! We're going to throw stones at her until she's dead.'

Jesus looked around the crowd and saw that quite a lot of them already had stones in their hands. His friend, John, had noticed that too. 'You'd better keep out of this one, Jesus,' he whispered. 'Otherwise, I'm afraid some of those stones might come in our direction.'

'What?' Jesus said. 'And let them stone this woman to death? I'm not going to stand by and let that happen.'

The crowd were getting impatient. 'Come on,' someone shouted. 'Let's get her outside the town and get on with it.'

But Jesus still stood in the way. 'Why do you want to do this?' he asked. 'What has she done?'

Josh grinned in an evil way. 'She's always breaking the law,' he said. 'No-one respects the law these days – so we're going to enforce it.'

'But who do you think you are?' asked Jesus.

'An honest, respectable citizen,' said Josh, with a self-satisfied look. Actually, he wasn't anything of the sort, but he had never been caught, so he thought that was all right!

Jesus still stood in the way. His friends were really getting anxious. 'He's going the right way about getting himself killed along with her,' muttered James, 'and us with him!'

'He's standing up for what's right,' said Thomas. 'I vote we stick with him.'

Jesus thought for a moment longer, and then said, 'I'll tell you what. If there's anyone among you who has never done anything wrong – anything at all, no matter how tiny – they can throw the first stone.'

Well! You could have heard a pin drop! Josh knew that, whatever he said to other people, he wasn't really as good as all that. After a few moments' thought, he let go of his stone, and it went clattering down the hill. Then someone else did the same, and then another, and soon the square was filled with the sound of stones rolling down the hill. And as they dropped their stones people turned and walked away, looking very embarrassed.

Eventually, the only people left were Jesus, his friends, and the woman, who was sitting on the floor, crying. Jesus spoke to her. 'No-one's having a go at you any more,' he said.

'No,' sobbed the woman, 'they aren't'

'Well,' said Jesus, 'I'm certainly not going to. Now you've got the chance to start again. You can be different from now on!'

The woman was so confused, and so relieved, that she just ran home!

'Well, Jesus,' said Philip, 'that was amazing! They just seemed to fade away after what you said to them.'

'Yes,' Jesus answered, 'when it comes to throwing stones at others, people often find that they're living in glass houses themselves!'

Our Story

Draw attention to the display. The class found something good in everybody – whether they were close friends or not. Perhaps we'd all be a lot happier if we looked for the good instead of the bad.

Prayers

We're Glad

You love us, Jesus,
whatever we're like:
when we're good,
and when we're not.
Thank you for all the people we know;
thank you for everything
that's good about them.
Help us to notice the good things

more than the bad.
We're Sad

We know we're not always kind.
We often think other people are worse
than they are,
and that we are better than we really are.
Jesus, help us to see
the good that's in others.
And when we start to say
how bad they are,
help us to remember
that we aren't perfect, either.

Let's Pray for People

Jesus, you love everybody.
We pray for people who think
that nobody loves them,
or who think that they are bad.
Help us to be kind to them.
Help us to show that we care,
and that you love them.

Songs

I'm black, I'm white, I'm short, I'm tall
Keep on travelling on
God is making a wonderful world

– from *Wake up, World!*

He's got the whole world in his hand
One more step along the world I go

– from *Come and Praise*

Jesus had all kinds of friends

– see *Appendix*

Living in Glass Houses

God's Story

Narrator   One day, Jesus and his friends heard a dreadful noise and saw a large crowd, dragging a frightened woman along. Jesus was horrified. But Matthew was a bit worried about getting involved.

Jesus   We've got to stop this. Look what they're doing to that poor woman.

Matthew   I'd be careful, if I were you. There may be a good reason for it.

Jesus   There's never a good reason to treat anyone like that! Whatever she's done, she's a human being.

Matthew   Well, I'd keep out of it. It's always best not to get involved.

Narrator   Jesus was going to say something very stern to Matthew, but by that time the crowd were really wound up!

- They were *rolling up their sleeves*
- They were *picking up stones*
- They were *taking aim*

So Jesus spoke to the mob leader – a nasty, vindictive character, called Josh.

Jesus   What on earth do you think you are doing?

Josh   We're going to throw stones at her until she's dead.

Matthew   You'd better keep out of this one, Jesus. They've all got stones in their hands, and I'm afraid some of them might come in our direction.

Jesus   What? And let them stone this woman to death?
I'm not going to stand by and let that happen.

Josh   I've had enough of this! Come on, let's get on with it.

Jesus   You'll have to get past me first! Why do you want to
do this, anyway?

Josh   *(with an evil grin)* She's always breaking the law –
so we're going to enforce it.

Jesus   But who do you think you are?

Josh   *(smugly)* An honest, respectable citizen.

Jesus   You mean you've never been caught! I'll tell you what,
Josh: if there's anyone among you who has never done
anything wrong – anything at all, no matter how tiny –
they can throw the first stone.

Narrator   Well! You could have heard a pin drop! Josh knew
that, whatever he said to other people, he wasn't really
as good as all that. After a few moments, he let go of
his stone and it clattered down the hill. Then someone
else did the same, and soon the square was filled with
the rolling stones (and we all know how deafening *that*
can be) down the hill. And as they dropped their
stones, people turned and walked away. Eventually,
only Jesus, his friends and the woman were left.

Jesus   Now you've got the chance to start again. You can be
different from now on!

Narrator   The woman was so relieved that she just ran home!

Jesus   You know, when it comes to throwing stones at others,
people usually find that they're living in glass houses
themselves!

I Can See!

Based on John 9:1-39

BEFORE THE DAY

Ask the children what they would miss most if they couldn't see. How would they attempt to make up for lack of sight? Prepare a tactile display, using objects with very different surfaces.

• Think about the actions for all the children to join in during the story.

ON THE DAY

Introduction

We're going to think about different kinds of blindness in a few moments. But first we'll say our 'Thank you' prayer.

'Thank you' Prayer

Thank you, God, for all you give us,
thank you for the earth and sea;
thank you, God, for special people,
thank you, God, for making me.

God's Story

Let me tell you about Tim. He was very clever. Some people said he could have been a good lawyer if he'd had the chance, but he never did. Instead, every day, he sat in the streets hoping people would put some money in the bowl beside him.

Tim's problem was that he'd been born blind. And in those days, that meant he couldn't go to school, or get a job. The rest of him worked well – his ears could hear, his nose could smell, his mouth could talk. It was just that his eyes couldn't see. And because of that one thing, everyone thought he was useless. Poor Tim!

One day, as Tim sat in the streets begging, Jesus and his friends walked past. Matthew said, 'I wonder why he's blind; his parents must have done something dreadful, and God's punishing them.'

'Perhaps he's the one who's being punished,' said John. 'After all, he's the one who's blind.'

'You don't really think God would do that, do you?' Jesus said. 'But as the man is blind, we can use him to show how much God loves people.'

Then Jesus did something very strange. He made some mud from the dust on the ground, and went over to smear it on Tim's eyes.

'Hey!' Tim shouted. 'What do you think you're doing – leave me alone – GERROFF!'

'Don't worry,' said Jesus, 'I'm not trying to hurt you. My name is Jesus, and I want to help you to see.' Then he told Tim to wash in a pond nearby. Tim didn't need to be told twice, and hurried to wash his face.
When he got to the pool . . .

• He *washed his face*
• He *blinked* in amazement
• He *jumped* for joy

'Hey, everybody,' he shouted, 'I can see! I can see people, and houses, and this must be a tree . . .'

Some important people heard the noise and came to see what it was all about. 'What's going on?' asked Paul, who was a lawyer, and a council member. 'What's all the fuss about?'

'I can see! I can see!' shouted Tim, excitedly.

'Don't be silly,' said Paul. 'You're blind – I've seen you begging.'

'Yes,' said Tim, 'but I can see now! Look, I can see a donkey over there, and there's a camel, and . . .'

'All right, calm down,' said Paul. 'How did this happen?'

'Well, it was the funniest thing,' explained Tim. 'This man called Jesus put some mud on my eyes and told me to wash. I thought he was barmy, I don't mind telling you – but now I can see!'

'That troublemaker Jesus again!' thought Paul. 'If this goes on, people will think that Jesus is more important than I am.' Then he turned to Tim. 'You're a liar,' he said. 'You just pretended to be blind to get easy money.'

'Don't be silly!' said Tim. 'The amount of money I got that way, I'd rather have worked.'

'All right, I believe you,' said Paul, 'but this is the day of rest. So if Jesus healed you today he must be an evil man.'

'Evil?' yelled Tim. 'How can someone who helps people be evil?'

Then some other lawyers said, 'Jesus can't have come from God, or we'd have known about him. We don't know who he is.'

'Well, there's a funny thing,' said Tim, laughing at them. 'You don't know who he is! Even I can see who he is. You clever lot can't see what's right in front of your noses – and to think, people used to say that *I* was blind!'

So Tim believed that Jesus was a special good person, from God, but the lawyers just carried on saying what a dreadful, wicked person he was. But then, as Tim used to say, there's none so blind as those who will not see!

Our Story

Would any children volunteer to be blindfolded, and see whether they can identify display items by touch alone? *If it can be done safely*, you might like to move some things around after the blindfolds are on, and then see if the children can find their way round the room.

Talk about things we sometimes don't see even when we do have our eyes open, like whether people are worried or unhappy.

Prayers

We're Glad

It's good to be able to see.
We can see flowers, and trees, and pictures.
Best of all, we can see each other.
We can see when people need us,
and that they love us.
Thank you, Jesus,
for helping us to see.

We're Sad

We don't always see things.
Sometimes people are worried or upset,
and we just don't notice.
We just carry on as though everything's fine,
and we don't see
that for some people it's not.
Jesus, when we're happy,
remind us about others.
And when we're sad,
don't let us forget that others are, too.

Let's Pray for People

We pray for people who can't see.
Help them to use other ways
– like hearing, or touching,
and help us to know
when they need a bit of help.

Songs

God is making a wonderful world
God made the earth
Out to the great wide world we go!

– from *Wake up, World!*

Jesus Christ is here
Think of a world without any flowers
Who put the colours in the rainbow?

– from *Come and Praise*

I Can See!

God's Story

Narrator Tim was very clever. But every day he sat in the streets begging. Tim had been born blind, which in those days meant he couldn't go to school, or get a job. The rest of him worked well – he could hear, smell, talk. It was just that he couldn't see. And because of that one thing, everyone thought he was useless. Poor Tim! One day Jesus and his friends walked past and Matthew asked Jesus a question.

Matthew Why's he blind, Jesus? Did his parents do something dreadful, and God's punishing them, or is he the one who's being punished?

Jesus You don't really think God would do that, do you?

Narrator Then Jesus did something very strange. He made some mud from the dust on the ground, and smeared it on Tim's eyes. Tim wasn't impressed at first!

Tim Hey! Leave me alone – GERROFF!

Jesus Don't worry. My name is Jesus, and I want to help you to see. Now go and wash in the pond over there.

Tim You bet I will – fancy doing a thing like that!

Narrator When Tim got to the pool . . .

- He *washed his face*
- He *blinked* in amazement
- He *jumped* for joy

Tim Hey, everybody, I can see!

Narrator	After a little while, some important people heard the noise and came to see what it was all about.
Tim	I can see! I can see!
Paul	Don't be silly! You're blind – I've seen you begging.
Tim	Yes, but I can see now! Look, I can see a donkey over there, and there's a camel, and . . .
Paul	All right, calm down! How did this happen?
Tim	Well, it was the funniest thing. This man called Jesus put some mud on my eyes and told me to wash. I thought he was barmy, I don't mind telling you – but now I can see!
Paul	*(Aside, to audience)* That troublemaker Jesus again! If this goes on, people will think that Jesus is more important than I am. *(To Tim)* You're a liar. You just pretended to be blind to get easy money.
Tim	Don't be silly! I'd be better off working!
Paul	All right, I believe you. But this is the day of rest. So if Jesus healed you today he must be an evil man.
Tim	Evil? How can someone who helps people be evil?
Paul	Jesus can't have come from God, or we lawyers would have known about him. We don't know who he is.
Tim	Well, there's a funny thing! You clever lot can't see what's right in front of your noses – and to think, people used to say that I was blind!

Dead and Alive Again

Based on the Passion and Resurrection Narratives

BEFORE THE DAY

What examples of new life can the children think of? Have the leaves appeared on the trees yet, following the 'death' of winter? Why not take the children out to see the signs of Spring? Ask them to bring flowers, eggs or other symbols to the assembly, and keep these things with them.

• Think about the actions for all the children to join in during the story.

ON THE DAY

Introduction

This morning, we're going to hear the story of Jesus being raised from the dead. But first we'll say our 'Thank you' prayer.

'Thank you' Prayer

Thank you, God, for all you give us,
thank you for the earth and sea;
thank you, God, for special people,
thank you, God, for making me.

God's Story

Not everyone liked Jesus. Some people liked to think they were important, and were afraid Jesus might get to be more important than they were. There were other people who didn't like what Jesus said. 'He wants us to be friends with bad people,' they would say, 'and with people who have skin diseases, and horrible things like that.'

So one day, some of these people (who thought they were good, but were really not nice at all) took Jesus to court and said nasty things about him. They even managed to frighten the judge, and get Jesus put to death. Jesus' enemies thought they'd won.

'That will teach people not to interfere in our religion,' said Jerry, one of the religious leaders.

'Yes,' said another, 'and it will stop all that stuff about God loving everybody – so now we can go on saying that God only loves people like us, and Jesus won't be here to argue about it.'

'I think we've done a good day's work, getting rid of him,' said Jerry.

What they didn't know, of course, was that they *hadn't* got rid of him, at all! Jesus was killed on the Friday. Then on the Sunday, Mary Magdalene said to her friends, Joanna and another Mary, 'Let's go to Jesus' grave. At the very least, we could put some flowers on it.'

Joanna wasn't sure. 'The government didn't like Jesus,' she said. 'Won't they be watching his grave, to find out who his friends are?'

But the other Mary said, 'They know about us, anyway. I agree with Mary – we should go and have a look.'

So there they were, very early on Sunday morning, going along to the grave where Jesus had been buried. When they got there, they found that the grave was empty.

They were very puzzled.

• They *scratched their heads*
• They *wrung their hands*
• They *peered all round*

Then they found someone waiting there, who said, 'It's no good looking for Jesus here – he's alive again, so what would he be doing in a grave?' Well, Joanna and Mary were terrified! They didn't know what was going on, but they knew they didn't like it very much! So they ran off, and didn't dare tell a single person what they had seen.

Mary Magdalene stayed, though. What was said hadn't sunk in, and she was still wondering what to do when she thought she saw the gardener. It was not really light yet, and she couldn't see very well, but she thought he looked like quite a kind person. So she said to him, 'I've come to find the grave where they buried Jesus, but it's empty. What have you done with him?'

Then the man said to her, in a very familiar voice, 'Mary!' It was Jesus! He *was* alive again!

'Teacher!' Mary called out and went to grab hold of him, but Jesus stopped her.

'Don't cling on to me,' he said. 'You can't just hang on to the past. We've got new things to do, now!'

'What shall I do, then?' asked Mary.

'Go and find the others,' said Jesus, 'and tell them that I'm alive.'

'Shall I bring them back here?' asked Mary.

'Oh no!' replied Jesus. 'I'm not going to hang around in this place for ever – I've got work to do.'

'So where will they find you?' asked Mary.

'Where they always have,' said Jesus. 'Out in the world. Wherever people are, there they'll find me.'

So Mary ran back and told the disciples what Jesus had said. 'He's alive,' she said, 'and no-one's ever going to be able to kill him again. He's going to be here forever, even when we can't see him, and he'll never leave us.'

And d'you know, she was quite right.

Our Story

Ask the children to bring their flowers or whatever they have to the front and make up a 'New Life' display. Speak with them about the hope which the renewal of the world brings.

Prayers

We're Glad

Thank you God,
for bringing Jesus back to life.
Thank you for promising
that he'll always be with us.

We're Sad

We're not always as good as we could be.
We don't actually kill people
when we're jealous of them,
but sometimes we hurt them,
or try to make them look silly.
And when we're unkind to them
we hurt Jesus as well.
We're sorry.
Please Jesus,
help us to be kinder
to one another.

Let's Pray for People

Let's pray for people who are sad
because someone has died.
Loving God,
even though we believe in heaven,
it still hurts when people die.
We miss them,
and we wish we could have them still with us.
Help people who are sad
because someone they love has died.
Help them to trust you,
and help us to understand them.

Songs

You can't pin Jesus down!
He was born in the winter
Out to the great wide world we go

– from *Wake up, World!*

Morning has broken
Jesus Christ is here
One more step along the world I go
He's got the whole world in his hand

– from *Come and Praise*

Come on and celebrate

– from *Songs of Fellowship*

Dead and Alive Again

God's Story

Narrator   Not everyone liked Jesus. Some people liked to think they were important, and were afraid Jesus might get to be more important than they were. Others didn't like what Jesus said. So one day, some of these people (who thought they were good, but were really not nice at all) said horrible things about Jesus and had him killed. Jesus' enemies thought they'd won. What they didn't know, of course, was that they *hadn't* got rid of him, at all! Jesus was killed on the Friday. Then on the Sunday, Mary Magdalene and her friends had an idea.

Mary   Let's go to Jesus' grave. We could put some flowers on it.

Joanna   I'm not sure. Won't the people who killed Jesus be watching his grave, to find out who his friends are?

Mary   So what? They know about us, anyway.

Joanna   I suppose you're right – I'd like to go.

Narrator   So they went together but when they got there, they found that the grave was empty. They were very puzzled.

- They *scratched their heads*
- They *wrung their heads*
- They *peered all round*

Then they noticed a stranger waiting there.

Stranger   It's no good looking for Jesus here – he's alive again, so what would he be doing in a grave?

Narrator Joanna was terrified! She didn't know what was going on, but she knew she didn't like it! So she ran off, but Mary Magdalene stayed. What was said hadn't sunk in, and she was still wondering what to do when she thought she saw the gardener. It was not really light yet, and she didn't recognise that it was Jesus.

Mary Excuse me, I've come to find Jesus' grave.

Jesus Mary!

Narrator It was Jesus! He *was* alive again! Mary went to grab him, but Jesus stopped her.

Jesus Don't cling on to me! You can't just hang on to the past. We've got new things to do, now! Go and tell the others that I'm alive.

Mary Shall I bring them back here?

Jesus Oh no! I'm not going to hang around in this place for ever – I've got work to do.

Mary So where will they find you?

Jesus Where they always have – out in the world. Wherever people are, there they'll find me.

Narrator So Mary ran back and told the disciples what Jesus had said.

Mary He's alive, and no-one's ever going to be able to kill him again. He's going to be here forever, even when we can't see him, and he'll never leave us.

Narrator And d'you know, she was quite right.

I'll Believe It When I See It

Based on John 20:24-29

BEFORE THE DAY

Prepare some pieces of paper with simple easily checked statements on them, some true and some false, such as 'John has red hair' or Emma has brown eyes' or 'This school is for girls only'. Have a board ready on which they can be pinned or stuck, divided into two halves marked 'True' and 'False'. Have some more statements which are less easy to check, such as 'Mount Everest is 8,848 metres high'. You could ask the class to contribute statements of their own.

• Think about the actions for all the children to join in during the story.

ON THE DAY

Introduction

We're going to hear a famous Easter story in a few moments, but first we'll say our 'Thank you' prayer.

'Thank you' Prayer

Thank you, God, for all you give us,
thank you for the earth and sea;
thank you, God, for special people,
thank you, God, for making me.

God's Story

After Jesus had risen from the dead, Mary Magdalene ran and told his friends all about it. But none of the men believed it. Whatever she said, Mary couldn't convince them that she'd seen Jesus. Then, as they were arguing, Jesus was suddenly standing among them! They were terrified!

• They *covered their faces*
• They *peeped between their fingers*
• Then they *covered their faces again*

They thought it must be a ghost – after all, the doors and windows were locked, and he couldn't have come down the chimney with the fire burning!

'Don't worry,' he said. 'I'm not a ghost. Here, come and take hold of my hand, just to prove that I'm real.'

Very gingerly, Peter took Jesus' hand. 'It's true!' he shouted. 'It really is him!'

Then everyone went wild! They all crowded round Jesus, trying to grab hold of him, and asking lots of questions. But Jesus stopped them. 'The important thing,' he said, 'is that God has brought me back to life. Your job is to go and tell everybody that – not waste time trying to work out how he did it!' Then, all of a sudden, he was gone! This really was very difficult for his friends. They'd never been too sure what Jesus was going to do next, before he had been killed. But now he seemed to be able to come and go as he liked.

'The fact is,' Peter said, 'no-one's ever been able to pin Jesus down, and we certainly can't now. He's not just alive, he's *free* as well!'

As he was speaking, Thomas came in. He'd been out visiting his brother and had missed all of the drama. He could tell that everybody was excited.

'What's going on?' he asked.

'Jesus has been here,' said John. 'He's alive.'

'Pull the other one!' said Thomas. No matter what they said, they couldn't convince him. 'I'll tell you what,' he said to them, 'if I can see him, and touch him, and touch the wounds on his body, then I'll believe he's alive. But until then I won't!'

'Why?' asked Philip. 'Don't you trust your own friends?'

'Not a lot,' said Thomas. 'Remember that time when you told me the easy way to count sheep?'

'What was that?' asked Mary Magdalene.

'Count the legs and divide by four!' said Andrew.

'And Thomas actually tried it!' said James, and everyone laughed – except Thomas.

'Laugh if you like,' he said, 'but you're not

catching me again. I'll believe it when I see it.' And with that, he went home.

Thomas didn't see the other friends again for a week. They were in the room where they usually met, and were chatting away about this and that when everything went quiet! Jesus had come into the room again, and Thomas was staring at him as though he'd seen a ghost.

'Come here, Thomas,' said Jesus. 'I've something to show you.' And he showed him the wounds where the nails had gone in, and where a soldier's spear had cut into his side. 'You see, Thomas, it really is true,' Jesus said, 'and I'm certainly no ghost. Come and touch me if you like, and you'll find that I'm real.'

Thomas didn't need to touch Jesus – he was overjoyed. 'It's true!' he said, looking around him in amazement. 'My master – alive!'

'You've seen me,' Jesus said, 'and now you can believe. It's going to be harder for people who don't see me. You've got to go and help them.'

Some of the disciples used to tease Thomas after that, because he had doubted what they had told him. I expect he probably said, 'You've got no room to talk – you didn't believe it, either, when the women told you. You had to see before you believed, just like me.'

And of course, he would have been quite right, wouldn't he?

Our Story

Read out the first set of statements and ask the children on which side of the board each one belongs. How did they know? Because they could easily check them out. Now read out the second set, and ask the children on which side of the board they each belong. How will the children decide? Presumably it would depend partly upon who told them. We can't always check things for ourselves; sometimes we just have to trust people. But of course, we're careful whom we trust!

Prayers

We're Glad

We're glad you're alive, Jesus,
and even though we can't see you
we believe you're here,
because you help us
to love one another.
Thank you, Jesus,
for loving us,
and for being here.

We're Sad

Sometimes, Jesus, when we're unkind,
other people find it hard to believe in you.
We're sorry.
Help us to be more like you,
so that other people will believe
that you're alive.

Let's Pray for People

We're unkind to Thomas:
we call him 'Doubting Thomas'.
Perhaps we should call him 'Honest Thomas'!
We pray for people who are unsure
about what they believe.
Help them to be honest,
help others to understand,
and help us to be honest as well.

Songs

You can't pin Jesus down
He was born in the winter
Keep on travelling on!
Out to the great wide world we go

– from *Wake up, World!*

Morning has broken
He's got the whole world in his hand
One more step along the world I go
Jesus Christ is here

– from *Come and Praise*

Come on and celebrate

– from *Songs of Fellowship*

I'll Believe It When I See It

God's Story

Narrator   After Jesus had risen from the dead, Mary Magdalene ran and told his friends all about it. But none of the men believed it. Then, as they were arguing, Jesus was suddenly standing among them! They were terrified!

- They *covered their faces*
- They *peeped between their fingers*
- Then they *covered their faces again*

They thought it must be a ghost! Then he spoke to them.

Jesus   Don't worry, I'm not a ghost. Here, come and take hold of my hand, just to prove that I'm real.

Narrator   Very gingerly, Peter took Jesus' hand.

Peter   It's true! It really is him!

Narrator   Then everyone went wild! They all crowded round Jesus, asking questions.

Jesus   The important thing is that God has brought me back to life. Your job is to go and tell everybody that – not argue about how he did it!

Narrator   Then, all of a sudden, he was gone! His friends had never been too sure what Jesus was going to do next. But now he seemed to be able to come and go as he liked.

Peter   No-one's ever been able to pin Jesus down. He's not just alive, he's *free* as well!

Narrator   Just then, Thomas came in. He could tell that everybody was excited.

Thomas	What's going on?
Philip	Jesus has been here; he's alive.
Thomas	Pull the other one!
Narrator	Peter and Philip simply couldn't convince him.
Thomas	I'll tell you what: if I can see him, and touch him, I'll believe he's alive. But not until!
Philip	Why? Don't you trust your own friends?
Thomas	Not a lot! Remember when you told me the easy way to count sheep was to count the legs and divide by four?
Philip	And you actually tried it!
Thomas	Laugh if you like, but you're not catching me again.
Narrator	With that, Thomas went home. A week later Jesus appeared again, and this time Thomas was there, and he was overjoyed!
Thomas	It's true! My master – alive!
Jesus	You've seen me, and now you can believe. It's going to be harder for people who don't see me. You've got to go and help them.
Narrator	Some of the disciples used to tease Thomas after that, because he had doubted what they had told him. I expect he probably said that they had no room to talk – they didn't believe it, either, when the women first told them. They had to see before they believed, just like Thomas.
	And of course, he would have been quite right, wouldn't he?

Come On, Cough Up!

Based on Matthew 18:21-34

BEFORE THE DAY

What are the children's favourite toys? Ask them to draw pictures of them. (Bringing them into school might be a little risky!)

• Think about the actions for all the children to join in during the story.

ON THE DAY

Introduction

We're going to hear about someone who was very kind, and someone else who was not at all kind! But first we'll say our 'Thank you' prayer.

'Thank you' Prayer

Thank you, God, for all you give us,
thank you for the earth and sea;
thank you, God, for special people,
thank you, God, for making me.

God's Story

Bart was a very rich man, who often helped out people who were poor. One day, he realised that one man – called Joel – owed him a million pounds. He didn't really mind, but he thought he should remind Joel. 'I just wonder whether you realise,' he asked, 'that you owe me a million pounds?'

Joel got very frightened. 'I'm sorry,' he pleaded, 'but one of my children is getting married, and my wife's ill. Please don't ask for it back yet.' Bart felt sorry for Joel.

'Look,' he said, 'why not just forget about it?'

'For how long?' asked Joel.

'Just forget about it,' said Bart kindly. 'Don't worry about paying me back, ever.'

Joel was amazed! 'Thank you ever so much,' he said. 'I'm really grateful to you.' And Joel went off, walking on air! 'I must find some way of showing how grateful I am,'

he thought. 'Perhaps I could buy him a present, if I had some money.'

Just then he saw his neighbour, Nick. Nick owed Joel fifty pounds.

'Er, Nick,' said Joel, 'you know that fifty pounds you owe me – I'm afraid I need it back.'

'I'm sorry,' said Nick, 'but I haven't got it. My father died, and I've got the funeral to pay for. I'll pay you as soon as I can.'

'Give me my money!' shouted Joel grabbing Nick by the throat. 'Come on, cough up!'

Nick was certainly coughing! 'All right,' he spluttered. 'I'll have to borrow it.'

'Just get it,' said Joel roughly. Then he went on his way, thinking, 'Won't Bart be pleased when he gets his present?'

Meanwhile Nick was very worried. He couldn't find anyone to help, until someone said, 'Why don't you ask Bart? He'll lend it to you.' So Nick went off to Bart's house.

'Of course, I'll lend you the money,' said Bart. 'Might I ask what it's for?' Nick told him the whole story, not realising that Bart knew Joel. 'What!' shouted Bart. 'Do you mean he attacked you over a fifty pound debt?' Then he sent for Joel.

Now a few days earlier, Joel would have knocked politely on Bart's door and waited to be invited in. But now, he thought it was different. He breezed in and said, 'Wotcha, Bart!'

'Get out and knock!' Bart bellowed. 'And don't come in until I tell you.' Joel ran outside and closed the door. He was scared stiff!

- His *hands* were *trembling*
- His *teeth* were *chattering*
- His *hair* was *standing on end*

It took him quite a few moments to pluck up the courage to knock.

Inside the room, Bart heard the knock and recited a little rhyme to himself:

'One, two, three, four,
let him sweat a little more.
Five, six, seven, eight,
bet he's getting in a state!'

Then he shouted, 'Come in – I'm waiting!'

Joel went in. 'What's this I hear about you being unkind to Nick?' asked Bart.

'I only asked for what he owes me,' said Joel.

'Asked him? Jolly near throttled him, from what I hear!' Bart corrected him.

'I only did it because I wanted to buy you a present to show my gratitude,' said Joel.

'So you show me you're grateful by bullying my friends, do you?' roared Bart. 'And to think I let you off a million pounds! Well, I want it back by next week.'

'What, all of it?' gulped Joel.

'Every single penny!' said Bart. 'And if you fail I've got a nice damp dungeon waiting for you.'

'I'll get it, I'll get it!' babbled Joel.

'Well don't get it by threatening any more people,' said Bart, 'or it will be worse for you!'

Poor old Joel. If only he'd been as kind to Nick as Bart was to him, he'd never have got into all that trouble, would he?

Our Story

Draw attention to the display. Would the children let others play with their favourite toys? What if they broke them? Emphasise that forgiveness doesn't absolve the other person of responsibility – as Joel found out!

Prayers

We're Glad

Thank you, God,
for being so good to us
even though we don't deserve it.
Thank you for people who are kind,
and who don't ask us
to repay their kindness.
But help us to do it, anyway,
by being kind to other people.

We're Sad

We're not always kind.
Sometimes we're quite cruel,
even though other people are kind to us.
We're sorry, Jesus,
help us to remember
how much you've forgiven us,
and that we should forgive others, too.

Let's Pray for People

Some people are very unhappy
because they can't forgive others.
They bear grudges,
and they keep reminding themselves
of how they've been hurt.
Help them to learn
that by forgiving people
they help make themselves happier, too.

Songs

Out to the great wide world we go!
God made the earth

– from *Wake up, World!*

When I needed a neighbour were you there?
God knows me

– from *Come and Praise*

Jesus had all kinds of friends

– see *Appendix*

Come On, Cough Up!

God's Story

Narrator   Bart was a very rich man, who often helped out people who were poor. One day, he realised that one man – called Joel – owed him a million pounds. He didn't really mind, but he thought he should remind Joel.

Bart   I just wonder whether you realise that you owe me a million pounds?

Joel   I'm sorry, but one of my children is getting married, and my wife's ill. Please don't ask for it back yet.

Bart   Look, why not just forget about it? Don't worry about paying me back, ever.

Joel   Wow! Thank you ever so much. I'm really grateful.

Narrator   Joel went off, walking on air!

Joel   I must find some way of showing how grateful I am. I could buy him a present, if I had some money.

Narrator   Just then Joel saw his neighbour, Nick. Nick owed Joel fifty pounds.

Joel   Er, Nick, you know that fifty pounds you owe me – I'm afraid I need it back.

Nick   I'm sorry, but I haven't got it. My father died, and I've got the funeral to pay for. I'll pay you as soon as I can.

Joel   (*Grabbing hold of Nick*) Give me my money! Come on, cough up!

Nick   All right, I'll have to borrow it.

Narrator   Nick was really worried, and decided to ask Bart for help.

Bart   Of course I'll lend you the money. Might I ask what it's for?

Narrator	Nick told Bart the whole story, not realising that Bart knew Joel!
Bart	What! Do you mean he attacked you over fifty pounds?
Narrator	Then Bart sent for Joel, who walked into the office without even knocking!
Joel	Wotcha, Bart!
Bart	*(Shouts)* Get out and knock! And don't come in until I tell you.
Narrator	Joel ran outside and closed the door. He was scared stiff!

- His *hands* were *trembling*
- His *teeth* were *chattering*
- His *hair* was *standing on end*

When he knocked, Bart recited a little rhyme to himself:

Bart	One, two, three, four, let him sweat a little more. Five, six, seven, eight, bet he's getting in a state! *(louder)* Come in – I'm waiting!
Bart	What's this I hear about you being unkind to Nick?
Joel	I only asked for what he owes me.
Bart	Asked him? Jolly near throttled him, from what I hear!
Joel	I only wanted to buy you a 'thank you' present.
Bart	What, by bullying my friends? And to think I let you off a million pounds! Well, I want it back by next week. And if you fail I've got a nice damp dungeon waiting for you.
Joel	I'll get it, I'll get it!
Narrator	Poor old Joel! If only he'd been as kind to Nick as Bart was to him, he'd never have got into all that trouble, would he?

Everyone Gets The Same

Based on Matthew 20:1-16

BEFORE THE DAY

What do the children think are the necessities of life? Perhaps you could get them to draw pictures of their homes, food, families etc. or to bring in some things which they think are essential, such as food packets etc. This might be quite a revealing exercise!

• Think about the actions for all the children to join in during the story.

ON THE DAY

Introduction

Jesus told a story about a man who was not only fair but generous too. And he told the story to show what God is like. We'll hear a story rather like it in a moment. But first we'll say our 'Thank you' prayer.

'Thank you' Prayer

Thank you, God, for all you give us,
thank you for the earth and sea;
thank you, God, for special people,
thank you, God, for making me.

God's Story

Jack was a farmer, and whenever anyone was looking for a job, they would hope Jack might give them one, because he was a good man to work for.

One particular day, Jack needed an extra worker to help with the harvest, and so he went into the market place. When he got there, he found several people waiting, hoping for work. 'What's you name?' he asked the first one.

'My name's Ben,' was the reply, 'and I'm looking for work for the day.'

'Right,' said Jack. 'Are you any good at harvesting corn?'

'Oh, I've done a lot of that,' said Ben.

'Then I'll pay you twenty pounds for the day,' said Jack, and they went off together.

At about lunch time, Ben said, 'I won't be able to get all this done by myself today; I'll need some help.'

So off Jack went, back to the market place. 'What's your name?' he asked the first man he came to.

'I'm Joe,' said the man. 'Nobody seems to have any work today, and I need the money to get myself a warm winter coat.'

'I'll pay you twenty pounds,' said Jack.

'Terrific!' said Joe, and they went back together.

At about three o'clock, Joe said, 'We really need some more help.' So Jack went to the market again. There was a woman there, looking very sad!

'No-one seems to have any work today,' she said. 'I'll never get my garden fence mended at this rate.'

'What's your name?' asked Jack.

'Dinah,' she said.

'Well, Dinah,' said Jack, 'I'll give you twenty pounds for the rest of the day.' Dinah agreed, and they went back together.

At the end of the day, Jack went out and called Ben, Joe and Dinah over. 'Thank you for your help, Dinah,' he said.

• He *shook her hand*
• and he *counted out her money*

'Here's your twenty pounds,' he said.

'Thank you very much,' said Dinah.

Then Jack came over to Joe. 'Thank you,' he said, 'you've done a really good job today.

• He *shook his hand*
• and he *counted out his money*

'Twenty pounds!' exclaimed Joe. 'But that Dinah woman got twenty pounds – and she'd only worked a couple of hours.'

Then Ben said, 'Joe's right. Dinah should get less than him, and he should get less than me, because I worked longest.'

'I don't know what you're so upset about,'

said Jack. 'You're going to get what we agreed – twenty pounds.'

'But you've given her the same,' yelled Ben, 'and she doesn't deserve it.'

'I never said that she deserved it,' said Jack. 'I don't care what she deserves – I'm only interested in what she needs.'

'Well!' said Joe. 'People think you're a fair man – they're wrong.'

'Yes, they are,' said Jack. 'Because I'm not being fair – I'm being generous, and that's quite different. Is it bad to be generous with my own money?'

As Ben and Joe left, grumbling, Jack's wife said, 'I think you've upset those two.'

'I know,' said Jack, 'but it's silly. If I'd only been fair, instead of generous, Joe couldn't have his new coat for the winter, and Dinah's garden fence would have to stay broken. How would that have helped Ben to feel better?'

As it was, Joe got his coat, Dinah got her fence repaired, and after a while Joe, Dinah and Ben became good friends, and often went to work for Jack together. Gradually, people stopped saying that Jack was 'very fair'. Instead, they used to say, 'He's very generous,' which was really much nicer, wasn't it?

Our Story

Point out the display. You might have some fun with the children about what they consider to be 'essential'! Show them that their parents provide what they need because they love them, and not because the children 'deserve' it. If they respond that their parents have to work for it, then that simply reinforces the parents' generosity toward the children. Jesus said that's what God is like.

Prayers

We're Glad

Thank you, Jesus,
for knowing what we need
and for caring about it.
Thank you for being not only fair
but generous!

We're Sad

Sometimes, Jesus, we're not nice to people
because we think they don't deserve it.
But you told us to be especially nice
to people we think are bad,
or who are not nice to us.
We're sorry that we haven't been
as generous as you.
Forgive us,
and help us to do better.

Let's Pray for People

Loving God
you care about people.
We pray for people who need clothes,
people who need houses,
people who need to be loved.
Help us to notice them,
and to do something to help.

Songs

We can plough and dig the land
I'm black, I'm white, I'm short, I'm tall
God is making a wonderful world
Out to the great wide world we go!

– from *Wake up, World!*

God knows me
He's got the whole world in his hand
When I needed a neighbour

– from *Come and Praise*

Everyone Gets The Same

God's Story

Narrator	Jack was a farmer who needed an extra worker to help with the harvest, and so he went into the market place.
Jack	What's your name?
Ben	My name's Ben and I'm looking for work for the day.
Jack	Right, are you any good at harvesting corn?
Ben	Oh, I've done a lot of that.
Jack	Then I'll pay you twenty pounds for the day.
Narrator	They went off together, and Ben started work. At about lunch time, Ben thought he'd better speak to Jack.
Ben	I won't be able to get all this done by myself today.
Narrator	So off Jack went, back to the market place.
Jack	What's your name?
Joe	I'm Joe. Nobody seems to have any work today, and I need the money to get myself a warm winter coat.
Jack	I'll pay you twenty pounds.
Narrator	So they went back together. But they still needed more help and Jack went back to the market.
Dinah	No one seems to have any work today. I'll never get my garden fence mended at this rate.
Jack	What's your name?
Dinah	Dinah.
Jack	I'll give you twenty pounds for the rest of the day.

Narrator   So Dinah joined Ben and Joe, and at the end of the day Jack went out and called them over. He thanked Dinah for her help.

- He *shook her hand*
- and he *counted out her money*

Dinah   Thank you very much.

Narrator   Then Jack came over to Joe.

- He *shook his hand*
- and he *counted out his money*

Joe   Twenty pounds! But that Dinah woman got twenty pounds – and she'd only worked a couple of hours.

Ben   Joe's right. Dinah should get less than him, and he should get less than me, because I worked longest.

Jack   I don't know what you're so upset about. You're going to get what we agreed – twenty pounds.

Ben   But you've given her the same, and she doesn't deserve it.

Jack   I never said that she deserved it. I don't care what she deserves – I'm only interested in what she needs.

Joe   That's not fair!

Jack   No, it's generous – and that's quite different. If I was fair, Joe couldn't have his new coat and Dinah's garden fence would stay broken. Would that make you feel better, Ben.

Narrator   As it was, Joe got his coat, Dinah got her fence repaired, and after a while they all became good friends. Gradually, people stopped saying that Jack was 'fair' and started calling him 'generous', which was really much nicer, wasn't it?

What Have You Done With My Money?

Based on Matthew 25:14-30

BEFORE THE DAY

What are the children good at? Why not produce a display of their work?

• Think about the actions for all the children to join in during the story.

ON THE DAY

Introduction

We'll be thinking about talents in a few moments. But first we'll say our 'Thank you' prayer.

'Thank you' Prayer

Thank you, God, for all you give us,
thank you for the earth and sea;
thank you, God, for special people,
thank you, God, for making me.

God's Story

David was very rich. One day, when he was going away, he called three of his workers, and said, 'I want you to increase my business while I'm away. Let's start with you, Chloe. What are you good at?'

'I can grow things,' said Chloe.

'Then why not open a garden centre?' said David. 'Here's ten thousand pounds to start you off.' Chloe went away, very excited, and David turned to Barney. 'Well,' he said, 'what would you do with five thousand pounds?'

'I could start a catering business,' Barney replied. 'There's a real need for that.'

'Good!' said David, and Barney went off to get started. Then David turned to the third worker. 'Phil,' he said. 'Here's two thousand pounds. What will you do?' Phil was scared to death. He thought that if he failed David would be really angry. So he just mumbled something about having to think about it. 'You make sure you do,' said David, and went away.

Chloe bought some land and ordered the things she would need. Phil watched her, and thought, 'She'll have lost all that money before David comes home.'

Barney bought a shop, and had it fitted out as a bakery. Then he ordered cooking pots and dishes.

Phil watched Barney, and thought, 'He'll soon have wasted all that money, and then he'll be in real trouble.'

Phil couldn't think what to do. 'Whatever I do will fail,' he thought, gloomily. Eventually, he decided to dig a hole and bury it all! 'I won't make any profit,' he thought. 'But at least I won't have wasted it, like those other two.'

So that's what he did:

• He *dug* a deep hole
• He *lowered* the money in
• He *patted* the earth over

Meanwhile, signs were appearing all over the town, saying 'Come to Chloe's for Cucumbers.' There were other signs, too, that said 'Barney's Better Caterers', (don't confuse this with the other BBC, though, will you?) Soon, people came from miles away to buy flowers from Chloe, or wedding cakes from Barney. They had to make the High Street one way to prevent camel jams!

When David came back, Chloe and Barney closed up and went to meet him. Phil dug up the money he'd buried. Somehow, he knew he was in trouble!

'Well,' said David. 'What have you done while I've been away?'

Chloe stepped forward. 'The garden centre's done really well,' she said, 'I've got your ten thousand pounds here, and another ten thousand as well.'

'Well done, Chloe,' said David. 'I'll make you a partner in my business. Well, Barney, how's the catering business?'

'Excellent, thank you,' said Barney. 'I've got your five thousand pounds, and I've made another five thousand as well.'

'Wonderful!' exclaimed David. 'I'm making you a partner in my business, too.' Then he turned to Phil and said, 'What did you finally decide on?' Phil was very frightened, and ashamed.

'Er . . . um . . . ah . . . that is, well, you see you're such a good businessman – and I knew you'd be angry if I lost your money, so I decided to play safe.'

'Out with it!' David roared. 'What have you done with my money?'

'N-n-nothing, sir,' stammered Phil. 'I kept it safe for you. Here it is.'

'Is that all you've done?' asked David. 'At the very least you could have put it in the bank and got some interest. You know I wouldn't have minded if you'd tried, and failed. But not even to try at all – there's no excuse for that.' Then he turned to Chloe. 'Could you use another couple of thousand?' he asked.

'You bet,' said Chloe. 'I could open a refreshment room.'

'Yes,' said Barney, 'and I could do the catering.'

So everyone was happy – except poor old Phil, that is. If only he'd realised that there's no shame in failing – only in not even trying!

Our Story

Talk about the things the children have achieved, and about the work and commitment which it involved. Do they sometimes feel afraid of failure? Phil wasn't criticised for failing, but for not trying! In any case, is not the greatest talent of all the ability to make others happy?

Prayers

We're Glad

Thank you, God,
for trusting us.
We can all do something
to make the world a better place.
Help us to trust you,
and to use whatever you've given us
to make other people happy.

We're Sad

There are lots of things we can do
to help other people:
We can smile,
we can listen,
we can cheer them up if they're sad,
all sorts of things.
But sometimes we don't do them,
because we're afraid of getting things wrong.
But even if we did,
at least they'd know we'd tried!
We're sorry, Jesus,
help us to trust you more.

Let's Pray for People

Some people are always nervous,
afraid of getting things wrong.
So they never really enjoy life,
they miss so much!
We pray for them, Jesus,
give them confidence,
and help us to show them
how important they are to us.

Songs

God is making a wonderful world
Pick up your feet and go!
Out to the great wide world we go!
We can plough and dig the land

– from *Wake up, World!*

Somebody greater
Who put the colours in the rainbow?

– from *Come and Praise*

What Have You Done With My Money?

God's Story

Narrator David was very rich. One day, when he was going away, he called three of his workers to a meeting.

David I want you to increase my business while I'm away. Let's start with you, Chloe. What are you good at?

Chole I can grow things.

David Then why not open a garden centre? Here's ten thousand pounds to start you off.

Narrator Chloe went away, and David turned to Barney.

David What would you do with five thousand pounds?

Barney I could start a catering business.

David Good!

Narrator Barney left, and David turned to the third worker.

David Phil, here's two thousand pounds. What will you do?

Narrator Phil was scared to death.

Phil Er . . . I'll have to think about it.

David You make sure you do. Well, good-bye everybody.

Narrator Chloe bought some land and Barney bought a shop. Phil watched thinking that they were going to waste all David's money. But he couldn't think what to do with his.

Phil Whatever I do will fail and I'll be in trouble. I know – I'll bury the money safely in the ground.

Narrator   So that's what he did:

- He *dug* a deep hole
- He *lowered* the money in
- He *patted* the earth over

Meanwhile, signs were appearing all over the town, saying 'Come to Chloe's for Cucumbers' and 'Barney's Better Caterers'. (Don't confuse this with the other BBC, though, will you?) Business boomed and they had to make the High Street one way to prevent camel jams! Eventually David came back.

David   Well, how have you done while I've been away?

Chloe   Really well. I've made ten thousand pounds profit.

David   Well done, Chloe! I'll make you a partner in my business. Well, Barney.

Barney   I've made another five thousand pounds profit.

David   Wonderful! I'm making you a partner in my business, too. Now, Phil, what about you?

Phil   Er . . . um . . . ah . . . that is, well, you see . . .

David   Out with it! What have you done with my money?

Phil   N-n-nothing, sir. I kept it safe for you. Here it is.

David   Is that all you've done? I wouldn't have minded if you'd tried and failed. But not even to try at all – there's no excuse for that. Chloe, could you use another couple of thousand?

Chloe   You bet! I could open a refreshment room.

Barney   Yes, and I could do the catering.

Narrator   Poor old Phil! If only he'd realised that there's no shame in failing – only in not even trying!

Neighbours

Based on Luke 10:30-35

BEFORE THE DAY

Ask the children where everyday things such as cotton, tea and rice come from. Make up a display using objects, packets, adverts etc. and covering as many different regions and countries as possible.

• Think about the actions for all the children to join in during the story.

ON THE DAY

Introduction

Jesus told a special story, to show us what 'Neighbours' really means. We're going to hear one like it in a moment, but first we'll say our 'Thank you' prayer.

'Thank you' Prayer

Thank you, God, for all you give us,
thank you for the earth and sea;
thank you, God, for special people,
thank you, God, for making me.

God's Story

There was once a young man called Stephen, who lived in Jerusalem. One day, he decided to go to the library at Jericho, to look at some books. There were lots of hills and caves along the lonely road, where robbers lived. One of them, a nasty man called Barabbas (whom you may have heard of before), saw Stephen coming and called his gang to attack. Stephen tried his best, of course. He caught Barabbas with the end of a stick, making his nose bleed, and he kicked another one on the shins. But it was no good. Very soon, poor Stephen was lying on the road, bruised, battered, and with all his money gone. He couldn't even crawl to the side of the road, out of the hot sun. Then he heard someone coming. It was a priest. 'Oh, good!' thought Stephen. 'He's sure to help me.'

'What's happened to you?' the priest asked.

(Stephen thought that was a silly question, and nearly said, 'I was out fishing and my boat sank,' but thought he'd better not be rude). 'I've been mugged,' he said. 'Can you help me?'

- The *priest looked all around*
- and he *scratched his head*
- and he *shrugged his shoulders*

'Terribly sorry,' he said. 'But you're all covered in blood, and I'm just going to a service, so I mustn't get dirty. Don't worry, there'll be someone else along. God bless you.' And he hurried away. Stephen could think of a few things to shout after him, but he decided to save his strength.

Then a different kind of minister came along. 'Well,' thought Stephen. 'Perhaps he'll help me.'

'I say,' said the minister. 'Have you had an accident?'

'No,' said Stephen, 'I've been mugged.'

'Oh dear!' exclaimed the minister. 'Are the robbers still around?' and he scuttled off along the road, glancing nervously around him. Stephen was very worried, now. The sun was hot, and it really looked as though he might die.

Then someone else came along and had a look. 'Oh, no!' thought Stephen. 'It's Tom, that Samaritan who sells second-hand donkeys.' Well, you could understand Stephen being worried. After all everyone knew that Samaritans hated Jews, and everyone also knew that you couldn't trust a second-hand donkey salesman. But Stephen got a surprise.

'Dear me!' said Tom. 'You look in a bad way. Don't worry – I'll help you.'

'But what about the robbers?' said Stephen.

'I expect they're long gone by now,' said Tom, 'and if they're not, they'd probably get me anyway.' He rummaged around and found a bottle of wine.

'Hey,' said Stephen. 'This is no time for

social drinking.'

'I'm not going to drink it,' said Tom. 'I'm going to clean your wounds with it; there's no water to be had around here.' Tom hadn't got a first aid kit, so he tore up his shirt to make bandages for Stephen's wounds. Then he said, 'Let's get you onto my donkey, and we'll find a hotel.'

'I can't afford any hotel,' said Stephen, 'and anyway, my mother will be worried.'

'Don't worry,' said Tom. 'It won't cost you anything, and I'll take a message to your mother.'

Tom took Stephen to the hotel and told them to look after him there until he was well. 'I'm often along this road,' he said. 'I'll pay you when I come back.' Then he said to Stephen, 'Now don't you worry; I'll tell your mother you're all right. And don't fret about the hotel bill – I've told them I'll pay it.'

Stephen could not believe what was happening. As Tom was leaving, he called out, 'Tom, are you *really* a Samaritan?'

'Yes,' answered Tom, 'I really am.'

There was a silence, and then Stephen, looking really puzzled, said, 'And are you *really* a second-hand donkey salesman?'

Our Story

Draw attention to the display, and point out how much we need people from all parts of the world. When we need people as much as we do, it doesn't make sense to be prejudiced against them!

Prayers

We're Glad

Thank you, Jesus,
for lovely surprises,
when people we thought were unfriendly
turn out to be good.
Thank you, Jesus,
for lovely surprises.

We're Sad

Jesus, we say we're your friends,
so people expect us to be friendly.
Sometimes they get bad surprises from us.
They think we'll be kind,
and we're cruel,
or they expect us to be generous,
and we're selfish.
Then we let them down,
and ourselves,
and we let you down too.
We're sorry, Jesus,
help us to be good friends,
and good neighbours.

Let's Pray for People

Some people feel lonely,
as though they haven't got any good neighbours.
Help them to know that you love them,
and teach us to be good neighbours.

Songs

I'm black, I'm white, I'm short, I'm tall
Jesus had all kinds of friends

– from *Wake up, World!*

When I needed a neighbour
Black and white
God knows me

– from *Come and Praise*

Thank you, O God, for all our friends

– see *Appendix*

Neighbours

God's Story

Narrator   There was once a young man called Stephen, who lived in Jerusalem. One day, he was walking to Jericho when he got mugged. Poor Stephen was left lying on the road, bruised, battered, and with all his money gone. Then he heard someone coming. It was a priest.

Priest   What's happened to you?

Stephen   Stephen thought that was a silly question, and nearly said, 'I was out fishing and my boat sank,' but thought he'd better not be rude.

Stephen   I've been mugged. Can you help me?

Narrator   The priest didn't seem very eager.

- He *looked all around*
- and he *scratched his head*
- and he *shrugged his shoulders*

Priests   Terribly sorry but I'm on duty, so I mustn't get dirty. Don't worry, there'll be someone else along.

Narrator   The priest hurried away. Then a different kind of minister came along.

Minister   I say, have you had an accident?

Stephen   No, I've been mugged.

Minister   Oh dear! Are the robbers still around?

Narrator	And the minister scuttled off along the road, glancing nervously around him. Stephen was very worried now and really thought he might die. Then someone else came along.
Stephen	Oh, no! It's Tom, that Samaritan who sells second-hand donkeys.
Narrator	In those days *everyone knew* that Samaritans hated Jews, and *everyone knew* that you couldn't trust a second-hand donkey salesman.
Tom	Dear me! You look in a bad way. Don't worry – I'll help you.
Stephen	But what about the robbers?
Tom	I expect they're long gone by now, and if they're not, they'd probably get me anyway.
Narrator	Tom rummaged around and found a bottle of wine.
Stephen	Hey! This is no time for social drinking.
Tom	I'm going to clean your wounds with it, not drink it! Now let's see what's the matter with you.
Narrator	Tom hadn't got a first aid kit, so he and tore up his shirt to make bandages. Then Tom took Steven to a hotel, and told them to look after him there until he was well.
Narrator	Stephen could not believe what was happening.
Stephen	Tom, are you *really* a Samaritan?
Tom	Yes, I really am.
Stephen	Amazing! *(Pause)* And are you *really* a second-hand donkey salesman?

Let's Have a Party!

Based on Luke 14:15-24

BEFORE THE DAY

Talk with the children about parties: what do they eat? Do they play games? Make a list of the important ingredients of parties – and whatever you do, don't forget to include guests!

• Think about the actions for all the children to join in during the story.

ON THE DAY

Introduction

Today we're going to hear a story about a really special party. But first we'll say our 'Thank you' prayer.

'Thank you' Prayer

Thank you, God, for all you give us,
thank you for the earth and sea;
thank you, God, for special people,
thank you, God, for making me.

God's Story

Mike and Sarah were a couple who loved to throw parties. The table would be loaded with food, and decorated with flowers, and they always had a band. Their parties were the talk of the neighbourhood, and people used to say that only a very special kind of fool would ever refuse an invitation from Mike and Sarah.

One evening, they decided to have another party. They invited their friends Joe and Elizabeth, and some others called Tim and Anna, as well as Eli who was a newcomer. They all said they would come.

So Mike and Sarah started getting the food ready. 'We'll have a fruit punch,' said Sarah.

'Yes,' said Mike, 'But be careful – not everyone's used to your punches!'

Well, the food was ready, and the table was set out, and the 'Bethany Blues Band' was playing gently at one end of the room.

• One of them was *playing a trombone*
• One was *playing a piano*
• Another was *playing the drums*

Mike and Sarah were really excited – but gradually when no-one came, they started getting worried.

'I hope they haven't forgotten,' said Sarah.

'I'll go and check,' said Mike.

So he went to Joe and Elizabeth's place. Elizabeth looked very embarrassed.

'I'm sorry,' she said. 'But we've just bought that bit of land next door to our garden, and it's full of weeds! We'll have to weed it.'

Mike wasn't pleased. 'I wish you'd told us before,' he said. 'We've gone to a lot of trouble.' Then he went to find Tim and Anna.

'I really am sorry,' said Tim, 'but we've just bought this lovely new puppy, and we can't leave him all on his own, can we? I hope you haven't gone to too much trouble.'

'Yes,' replied Mike, '*much* too much trouble!'

And he went on to find Eli. 'Eli's probably forgotten,' he thought to himself. 'I expect he'll come back with me.' But when he got to Eli's house, no-one was in. Then one of the neighbours called out, 'Eli's off on his honeymoon – he got married this morning.'

Sarah was as angry as Mike was. 'D'you mean to tell me that they let us do all this work, and didn't really want to come at all?' she said. 'Well, someone's got to eat this food; it mustn't be wasted.'

'I know!' said Mike. 'If the people who were invited don't appreciate our cooking, let's invite those who will! Let's go into the streets, and invite all the homeless people – all the people nobody wants!'

'What a wonderful idea!' exclaimed Sarah. 'They'll appreciate a party, even if our boring friends don't!'

So that's what they did, and before long the house was full of people eating, and laughing, and singing and dancing. 'Well!' said Sarah. 'This is a bit different from our usual parties. No airs and graces – just people who appreciate a good party.'

'Yes!' said Mike. 'Even the band are enjoying it more than usual – just listen to how they're playing!'

Just then, Joe and Elizabeth arrived. 'We felt so sorry for you,' said Joe, as they swept in, 'that we put off the weeding and came. After all what are friends for?' Before Mike could answer, they had arrived in the dining room.

'Good grief!' screeched Elizabeth. 'What are all these people doing here?'

'Enjoying themselves, actually,' said Sarah. 'They really know how to get stuck in to a good party. Why don't you join them?'

'Not likely!' replied Elizabeth. 'Come on Joe, we're going home!'

The party continued well into the night. No-one wanted it to end. As they left the guests all said, 'When's the next party going to be?'

'As soon as possible,' smiled Sarah.

'Too right!' said Mike. 'I've never enjoyed anything so much!'

Our Story

Draw attention to the display. The food and other things are wonderful – but they're a lot better when there are people to share them with!

Prayers

We're Glad

Loving God,
thank you for fun,
for our family
and the things we enjoy together.
Help us to make each other happy.

We're Sad

Sometimes people go to a lot of trouble
to make us happy,
and we hurt them.
We're sorry, Jesus,
help us to be more careful
about other people's feelings.

Let's Pray for People

Some people are so sad,
and never really enjoy life.
They don't notice
the good things others do.
Other people spend lots of time
trying to make others happy,
and then feel let down.
We pray for them.
Help them to know that you care,
and that we care.
Show us how to make them feel
that all their work is worthwhile.

Songs

Jesus had all kinds of friends
I'm black, I'm white, I'm short, I'm tall
Jesus turned the water into wine

– from *Wake up, World!*

Come on and celebrate!

– from *Songs of Fellowship*

All things bright and beautiful
Jesus Christ is here
When I needed a neighbour

– from *Come and Praise*

Thank you, O God, for all our friends

– see *Appendix*

Let's Have a Party!

God's Story

Narrator   Mike and Sarah decided to have a party. They invited their friends Joe and Elizabeth, and some others called Tim and Anna, as well as Eli, who was a newcomer. They all said they would come. So Mike and Sarah started getting the food ready.

Sarah   We'll have a fruit punch.

Mike   Yes, but be careful – not everyone's used to your punches!

Narrator   Well, the food was ready, and the table was set out, and the 'Bethany Blues Band' was playing gently at one end of the room.

- One of them was *playing a trombone*
- One was *playing a piano*
- Another was *playing the drums*

Narrator   Mike and Sarah were really excited – but no-one came.

Sarah   I hope they haven't forgotten.

Mike   I'll go and check.

Narrator   First Mike went to see Joe and Elizabeth.

Elizabeth   I am really sorry but we've just bought a bit of land and we've got to weed it.

Mike   I wish you'd told us before.

Narrator   Then Mike went to find Tim and Anna.

Tim   I really am sorry but we've just bought this lovely new puppy, and we can't leave him all on his own, can we?

Narrator   When Mike got to Eli's house, no-one was in. Eli had got married and gone off on his honeymoon! Sarah was angry.

Sarah   Well, someone's got to eat this food; it mustn't be wasted.

Mike   I know! Let's invite all the homeless people, all the people nobody likes! They'll appreciate a party, even if our boring friends don't!

Narrator   Before long, the house was full of people having a wonderful time.

Sarah   Well! This is a bit different from our usual parties. No airs and graces – just people who appreciate a good party.

Narrator   Just then, Joe and Elizabeth arrived.

Elizabeth   We felt so sorry for you that we put off the weeding and came. After all what are friends for?

Narrator   Before Mike could answer, they had swept into the dining room.

Elizabeth   (*horrified*) Good grief! What are all *these* people doing here?

Sarah   Enjoying themselves, actually! Why don't you join them?

Elizabeth   (*snobbishly*) Not likely! Come on Joe, we're going home!

Narrator   The party continued well into the night. No-one wanted it to end. And I hear they're planning another – very soon!

What A Silly Sheep!

Based on Luke 15:1-7

BEFORE THE DAY

Think of the people on whom we rely to help us if we're in difficulties – even when it's our own silly fault! Perhaps the children could draw pictures of nurses, firemen, doctors etc. If some were able to dress up for the assembly, so much the better.

If using the drama, prepare some placards saying:

> This Way to Adventure

> Juicy Grass Over Here

• Think about the actions for all the children to join in during the story.

ON THE DAY

Introduction

In a few minutes, we're going to hear a sheep telling a story! But first we'll say our 'Thank you' prayer.

'Thank you' Prayer

Thank you, God, for all you give us,
thank you for the earth and sea;
thank you, God, for special people,
thank you, God, for making me.

God's Story

I never meant to cause trouble. I just wanted some excitement. Being a sheep isn't easy, you know – we spend most of our time travelling about looking for decent grass. The only view we get is the back of the sheep in front, and take it from me, that's not very exciting!

But we're lucky in one way – our shepherd's good. Joshua's his name. Not all the *people* like him, but then people are funny that way, aren't they? He's very popular with the sheep. He really cares about us – and a good thing too, or I would have got myself in big trouble by now!

I was always a bit of a rebel – always wandering off looking for excitement. My mum used to get so mad! 'One day,' she used to say to me, 'you'll get into real trouble!' I never believed her. I just longed to be big enough to go off on my own without her fussing over me. Then one day we'd stopped for a feed on some juicy grass, and I could see some that was even greener, just up the hill. So off I went, and no-one noticed. It was good stuff. Then I went further, and it was even better. The trouble was that I soon got lonely. I missed my mum and dad, and all my sisters and my cousins and my aunts in the flock. But when I tried to get back, I must have taken a wrong turning. It was all different. I thought I'd better try in another direction. But then I got completely lost!

I was getting frightened (but don't tell my mum I said that, will you, because she'd only say, 'I told you so!') and I began to think that I'd never get back. All this excitement was getting me down – and walking along looking at the rear view of another sheep seemed like a wonderful idea! As night fell, I thought I'd better try and find a cave to shelter in. So I tried to turn around and had the fright of my life. Somehow, I'd wandered onto the side of a cliff. I was standing on a ledge so narrow there was no way I could turn round. Now I was *really* frightened!

• I couldn't *fly* up to the top,
   'cos sheep can't *fly*
• I couldn't *climb a rope,*
   even if I'd had one!
• I couldn't *hang glide,*
   'cos I didn't have the gear!

Then, I heard a whistle; Joshua's special whistle he used when we wandered off. If I hadn't been standing where I was, I'd have jumped for joy. As it was, I just gave out a little 'Baa' and I heard the whistle again – this time closer than before. So I gave him another 'Baa!' And that's how we went on – whistle . . .

'Baa' . . . whistle . . . 'Baa' until he was at the cliff top above me.

'You wait there,' he called – as if I'd do anything else – 'and I'll be down to you.' He scrambled down to where I was. 'I don't know how you got here,' he said, 'but I'll get you safe.' And he picked me up, slung me across his shoulders and climbed up. I tell you, I closed my eyes and hung on. That was another thing my parents found embarrassing about me – a sheep that's scared of heights, I ask you!

When we got to the top, I thought Joshua was going to carry me all the way home on his shoulders, but he put me down. 'Come on,' he said. 'You walked here, you can walk home. But don't worry, I'll be right with you all the way.' And he was, too.

Since that day, I've been more careful. It's not so bad, travelling – in fact, we see some pretty exciting places. All I have to do is turn my head to the side – can't imagine why I didn't think of it before!

Our Story

Draw attention to the display. All those people will help us, because they care – even if it is our own fault! Of course, we should be careful not to waste their time, but everyone does silly things sometimes and it's good to know that someone will help us. Jesus told us that God is even more loving!

Prayers

We're Glad

Thank you, God, for caring for us.
Thank you for telling us that wherever we go,
and whatever we do, you won't forget about us

We're Sad

We know you care about us, Jesus,
and we know we should follow you.
But sometimes, other things seem more exciting,
and we wander off, do our own thing,
then complain when we get into trouble!
Help us to enjoy life, to have fun,
but to stay with you.

Let's Pray for People

People get lost sometimes,
and then others worry about them.
Loving God,
be very close to anxious people:
children who are lost,
parents who are worried about them,
people who have lost their way.
Thank you for people who help:
the police,
the Salvation Army,
and many other organisations.
Help them to go on showing
that you care.

Songs

Pick up your feet and go!
Out to the great wide world we go!
Keep on travelling on!
God made the earth

– from *Wake up, World!*

Come on and celebrate

– from *Songs of Fellowship*

He's got the whole world in his hand

– from *Come and Praise*

Thank you, O God, for all our friends

– see *Appendix*

What A Silly Sheep!

God's Story

Sheep   I never meant to cause trouble. I just wanted some excitement. Being a sheep isn't easy, you know – we spend most of our time following Joshua around (Joshua's our shepherd), looking for decent grass. I suppose I was always a bit of a rebel – always wandering off looking for excitement. My mum used to get so mad!

Placard holders   Over here! – No, over here! – Come this way! (*As they call, the Sheep starts towards each one*)

Mum   One day, you'll get into real trouble!

Sheep   See what I mean? Parents! I just longed to be big enough to go off on my own without her stopping me.

Placard holders   Over here! – No, over here! – Come this way!

Mum   You'll learn the hard way – you just mark my words!

Sheep   Yeah, yeah! Now where was I? Oh yes . . . One day I saw some juicy grass, just up the hill.

Placard holders   Over here! – No, over here! – Come this way!

Sheep   So off I went, and no one noticed. It was good stuff. And further on, it was even better. But I forgot to keep an eye on the others, and soon I was completely lost! I was very frightened (but don't tell my mum I said that, will you, because you know what she'd say . . .)

Mum   I told you so! I don't like to say it, but . . .

Sheep See what I mean? But I must admit that all this excitement was getting me down – and walking along back with the rest of the flock seemed like a wonderful idea! Then I had the fright of my life. Somehow, I'd wandered onto the side of a cliff and I was standing on a narrow ledge. Now I was *really* frightened!

- I couldn't *fly* up to the top, 'cos sheep can't *fly!*
- I couldn't *climb a rope*, even if I'd had one!
- I couldn't *hang glide*, 'cos I didn't have the gear!

Then, I heard something.
(*'Joshua' blows a whistle from the back of the hall*)
That was Joshua's special whistle he used when we wandered off. If I hadn't been standing where I was, I'd have jumped for joy. As it was, I just gave out a little 'Baa' and I heard the whistle again – this time closer than before. So I gave him another 'Baa!' And that's how we went on – whistle . . . 'Baa' . . . whistle . . . 'Baa' (*'Joshua' progresses gradually towards the front, still blowing the whistle when appropriate*) until he found me.

Joshua You wait there.

Sheep I ask you! As if I'd do anything else! He scrambled down to where I was and then he carried me up. I tell you, I closed my eyes and hung on. That was another thing my parents found embarrassing – a sheep that's scared of heights, I ask you! When we got to the top, Joshua put me down.

Joshua Come on! You walked here, you can walk home. But don't worry, I'll be right with you all the way.

Sheep He was, too. I'm more careful now. It's not so bad staying with the flock – in fact, we see some pretty exciting places. All I have to do is turn my head to the side – can't imagine why I didn't think of it before!

Whatever You've Done, I Love You!

Based on Luke 15:11-32

BEFORE THE DAY

How many reasons can the children think of for having a celebration? It might be a birthday, a success, someone getting better from an illness, or many other things. Write them up and get the children to illustrate them.

• Think about the actions for all the children to join in during the story.

ON THE DAY

Introduction

Jesus told a story about a man who thought he'd lost his son for ever, but got him back. We're going to hear a story like that, soon. But first we'll say our 'Thank you' prayer.

'Thank you' Prayer

Thank you, God, for all you give us,
thank you for the earth and sea;
thank you, God, for special people,
thank you, God, for making me.

God's Story

Jonathan was a young man who lived with his father, Sam, and his older brother, Enoch. Enoch was very serious and worked hard, but Jonathan just liked having fun.

One day, Jonathan said to Sam, 'I don't want the farm, but I'd like my share of your money. Why not give it to me now, while I'm young enough to enjoy it?'

Sam wasn't sure that would be a good idea, but he thought, 'He's a man now – he's got to make his own life.' So he said, 'Alright, that's your share. Use it well.'

'Oh I will!' said Jonathan. And he left. Just like that.

Jonathan knew of a country a long way away where everybody had fun. So he set off as fast as he could go.

Well, Jonathan had never known such parties! Everyone wanted to know this rich young man! Every night he was at parties, and he spent most of the day sleeping. But that didn't matter, because he was so rich he didn't need to work.

He went to the tailor and bought thirty suits, one for every night of the month. Then he found the games room. They didn't have slot machines in those days – they used people to take you money from you! Jonathan loved playing.

• He *dealt the cards*
• He *shook the dice*
• He *spun the wheel*

Jonathan never noticed how much money he was losing, until one day he went to get some money from his bag and had a dreadful shock – there were only a couple of pounds left! He'd gone through his entire fortune!

Jonathan thought long and hard about what to do. 'I've got lots of friends,' he thought. 'They will help me.' That was his second shock. No-one would help. Then the word got around that Jonathan was broke, and his friends disappeared. He sold his lovely clothes back to the tailor, but for a tenth of what he'd paid for them.

Soon, he was scruffy and dirty, and no-one wanted him. The only job he could get was as a pig-man. And he still couldn't afford food. 'I'll end up eating the pigswill at this rate,' he thought. Then he had an idea: 'My father pays his workers well. I wonder if he'd give me a job?' So he got up and started the long journey home.

On the way, he planned his speech. 'I'm sorry Dad,' he would say. 'I don't deserve to be your son any more. Can you give me a job? I'll work really hard this time, I promise.'

Sam was on the rooftop, where he'd been every day, hoping to see Jonathan coming back. When he saw his son, he ran and gave him a big hug. Jonathan never got the chance to say what he'd planned. His father called a servant. 'Look who's here!' he said, 'Go and get him some decent clothes – and organise a feast!'

Jonathan's brother Enoch heard the noise and asked what was happening 'We're having a celebration,' said a servant. 'Jonathan's back.'

Enoch was hopping mad! 'What are you doing,' he shouted at Sam. 'I've worked for you all these years for nothing, and now this lousy son of yours comes home and you have a celebration!'

Sam said, 'He's your brother, you know, as well as my son. You know you can have anything you want from me. But Jonathan seemed to be gone for good, and now he's back. Won't you come and celebrate with us?'

'Not on your life!' said Enoch.

There was a wonderful feast that night, but Enoch just stood outside, listening to the sounds. Deep down, he wanted to go in, but he was jealous. So he sulked, and made himself even more unhappy.

Wasn't that a shame?

Our Story

Show the group the display, and see if they can suggest any more reasons for having a party. Perhaps there doesn't need to be a reason! But if there is, it will almost always have something to do with people.

Prayers

We're Glad

Heavenly Father,
thank you for loving us.
Thank you for the people
who love us, (especially . . .)
We try to do the things
that will please you,
because we love you.
But even when we get things wrong,
you still love us. Thank you.

We're Sad

We get angry with people, sometimes.
Sometimes, we're so angry
that when they say 'sorry', we ignore them.
Then we make ourselves unhappy,
as well as them.
We're sorry that we can't love people
as much as you do.
Help us to be like Jonathan's father,
and not like his older brother.

Let's Pray for People

Let's pray for people who are angry,
so angry that it hurts.
Loving God,
help people who are angry.
Perhaps they have a good reason.
Perhaps they've been badly hurt.
But help them to forgive,
the way you do,
so that they can be happy themselves.

Songs

Jesus had all kinds of friends
Out to the great wide world we go!

– from *Wake up, World!*

God knows me
He's got the whole world in his hand

– from *Come and Praise*

Come on and celebrate

– from *Songs of Fellowship*

Whatever you've done, I love you!
Thank you, O God, for all our friends

– see *Appendix*

Whatever You've Done, I Love You!

God's Story

Narrator   Jonathan was a young man who lived with his father, Sam, and his older brother, Enoch. Enoch was very serious and worked hard, but Jonathan just liked having fun. One day, Jonathan asked Sam for a favour.

Jonathan   I don't want the farm, but I'd like my share of your money. Why not give it to me now, while I'm young enough to enjoy it?

Sam   I suppose you're a man now – you've got to make your own life. Alright, here's your share. Use it well.

Jonathan   Oh I will!

Narrator   Jonathan knew of a country a long way away where everybody had fun. So he set off as fast as he could go. When he arrived, everyone wanted to know this rich young man! Every night he was at parties. And then he found the games room. They didn't have slot machines in those days – they used people to take you money from you! Jonathan loved playing.

- He *dealt the cards*
- He *shook the dice*
- He *spun the wheel*

Jonathan never noticed how much money he was losing, until one day he went to get some money from his bag and had a dreadful shock – there were only a couple of pounds left! He'd gone through his entire fortune! What should he do now?

Jonathan   I've got lots of friends who will help me.

Narrator   But when word got around that Jonathan was broke, his friends disappeared. He had to take a job as a pig-man. And he still couldn't afford food.

Jonathan   I'll end up eating the pigswill at this rate! Just a minute, though; my father pays his workers well. I wonder if he'd give me a job?

Narrator   Jonathan started the long journey home.

Jonathan   Now, what shall I say when I get there? 'I'm sorry Dad, I don't deserve to be your son any more. Can you give me a job – I'll work really hard this time, I promise.' Yes, that's about right.

Narrator   When Sam saw his son coming home, he ran and gave him a big hug. Jonathan never got the chance to say what he'd planned. His father called a servant.

Sam   Look who's here! Let's celebrate!

Narrator   Jonathan's brother Enoch was hopping mad!

Enoch   What are you doing? I've worked for you all these years for nothing, and now this lousy son of yours comes home and you have a celebration!

Sam   He's your brother, you know, as well as my son. Won't you come and celebrate with us?

Enoch   Not on your life!

Narrator   There was a wonderful feast that night, but Enoch just stood outside, listening to the sounds. Deep down, Enoch wanted to go in, but he was jealous. So he sulked, and made himself even more unhappy. Wasn't that a shame?

Don't Just Sit There

Based on Acts 3:1-10

BEFORE THE DAY

Ask the children to imagine they couldn't use their legs. List the places they couldn't go, either in the school or in the community. Think of simple things which we take for granted. How good is the building for disabled people, and what needs to be changed? All this can form the basis for a display of writing and/or drawings.

• Think about the actions for all the children to join in during the story.

ON THE DAY

Introduction

We're going to hear a story soon, about a man who was always left out because he couldn't walk. But first we'll say our 'Thank you' prayer.

'Thank you' Prayer

Thank you, God, for all you give us,
thank you for the earth and sea;
thank you, God, for special people,
thank you, God, for making me.

God's Story

Have your legs ever felt like jelly – perhaps because you were frightened? Well, Jamie's legs were always like that. The rest of his body was fine, and his brain was great – but his legs wouldn't work at all! And long ago, when this story took place, you needed legs even more than you do now. There were no wheelchairs, and there seemed to be steps everywhere. So it was even more difficult for disabled people than it is now.

Every day, Jamie's friends carried him to the temple in Jerusalem and sat him down by the 'Beautiful Gate' where he could beg. Jamie hated it! It was so embarrassing! 'Why

should I have to do this?' he used to think. 'I've got a first class brain, and I can use my hands, but you'd think I was completely useless, just because my legs won't work!'

What sort of things do you think Jamie could do?

- Perhaps he could *paint pictures*
- Maybe he could *play a trumpet*
- Or *use a hammer*

But no one thought of that!

At about three one afternoon, Peter and John were going to the temple to worship God. Jesus had gone back to heaven, but he'd said he'd always be with them although they couldn't see him. He'd also given them jobs to do. So Peter and John were making plans.

'We must tell everybody about Jesus,' John was saying.

'The point is,' Peter said, 'that Jesus has shown us what God is like. If people knew that God was like Jesus, they'd love him more and be less frightened of him.'

'Yes,' said John, 'but how do we show them that?'

'We must let Jesus use our hands to help people,' Peter replied. 'And our mouths to speak to them'

'Fine,' said John, 'but first, we've got to let him use our ears to listen to them. That man over there, for example – what's he saying?'

They went over to Jamie. 'What do you want?' said John.

Jamie thought, 'They must be deaf!' Out loud, he said, 'I need money.'

'I know you need money,' said Peter. 'But what do you *really want?*'

'Oh, that's different! said Jamie. 'I want to be able to stand up on these silly legs. I want to be able to talk to people without their bending down to me as if I were a baby in a pram! I want to be able to walk into that temple on my own two legs – I want to run, and jump, and kick a ball like anyone else. I want . . .'

'Yes, I get the picture!' laughed John. 'You want good legs.'

'Fat chance of that, though,' said Jamie. 'So money will have to do.'

'Well, we haven't got any money,' said Peter. Jamie was really disappointed, but before he could speak, Peter went on, 'But I can give you something else: in the name of Jesus, stand up.'

Before Jamie could ask what was going on, he felt his toes tingling. He couldn't understand it. Then the tingling spread – up to his ankles, then to his knees, until the whole of each leg was burning. And what do you do if you burn your foot? You jump around a bit! So that's what Jamie did! Then he realised. 'Wow!' he said, 'What happened?'

'God made your legs better,' said John.

'Well, we'd better go and thank him!' shouted Jamie, and dragged Peter and John into the temple. Everyone was amazed to see him there.

Peter and John were pleased, too. 'That's because we did what Jesus would have done,' said John.

'You mean, by healing his legs?' asked Peter.

'No,' said John, 'by listening to what he *really* wanted. Just think, if we'd had any money to give him, he might still be sitting there!'

Our Story

Refer to the display, and tell the rest of the group how your class prepared for the assembly. Maybe the children can't change the building or community very easily (or there again, who knows . . .), but they can now be more sensitive to the needs of others, which is the real value of the exercise.

Prayers

We're Glad

Thank you, loving God,
for teaching people to listen.
Thank you for caring
about our real needs.
Thank you for helping us
to care for others
in the same way.

We're Sad

There are times when we don't listen.
Sometimes, we think we know best
what someone else needs.
Sometimes, we treat disabled people
as though they were invalids.
And they're not!
We're sorry if we hurt people,
please help us to listen
the way you do.

Let's Pray for People

Some people just don't get listened to.
They may be given things,
they may even be cared for,
but they don't get listened to.
Please God, help people to listen.
And when we've listened,
show us how we can help.

Songs

Pick up your feet and go!
God made the earth

– from *Wake up, World!*

One more step along the world I go
God knows me
Jesus Christ is here

– from *Come and Praise*

Stand up! Walk tall!

– see *Appendix*

Don't Just Sit There

God's Story

Narrator   Have your legs ever felt like jelly – perhaps because you were frightened? Well, Jamie's legs were always like that. The rest of his body was fine, and his brain was great – but his legs wouldn't work at all! Every day, Jamie's friends carried him to the temple in Jerusalem and sat him down by the 'Beautiful Gate', where he could beg. Jamie hated it! It was so embarrassing!

Jamie   I've got a first class brain, and I can use my hands, but you'd think I was completely useless, just because my legs won't work!

Narrator   What sort of things do you think Jamie could do?

- Perhaps he could *paint pictures*
- Maybe he could *play a trumpet*
- Or *use a hammer*

Narrator   But no-one thought of that! One afternoon, Peter and John were going to the temple. Jesus had gone back to heaven, but he'd said he'd always be with them although they couldn't see him.

John   We must tell everybody about Jesus.

Peter   The point is that Jesus has shown us what God is like. If people knew that God was like Jesus, they'd love him more and be less frightened of him.

John   Yes, but how do we show them that?

Peter   We must let Jesus use our hands to help people.

John   Fine, but first, we've got to let him use our ears to listen. That man, for example – what's he saying?

Peter   Let's ask him. What do you want?

Jamie	*(Aside to audience)* They must be deaf! *(To Peter)* I need money.
Peter	I know you need money, but what do you *really want?*
Jamie	Oh, that's different! I want to be able to stand up on these silly legs. I want to be able to talk to people without their bending down to me as if I were a baby in a pram! I want to be able to walk into that temple on my own two legs – I want to run, and jump, and kick a ball like anyone else. I want . . .
John	Yes, I get the picture! You want good legs.
Jamie	Fat chance of that, though, so money will have to do.
Peter	Well, we haven't got any money, but I can give you something else: in the name of Jesus, stand up.
Narrator	Before Jamie could ask what was going on, he felt his toes tingling. Then the tingling spread, until the whole of each leg was burning. And what do you do if you burn your foot? You jump around a bit! So that's what Jamie did!
Jamie	Wow! What happened?
John	God made your legs better.
Jamie	Well, we'd better go and thank him!
Narrator	Jamie dragged Peter and John into the temple. Everyone was amazed to see him there.
John	That happened because we acted like Jesus.
Peter	You mean, by healing his legs?
John	No, by listening to what he *really* wanted. Just think, if we'd had any money, he might still be sitting there!

WE'RE ALL GOING TO THE PROMISED LAND

Text: Michael Forster
Music: Christopher Tambling

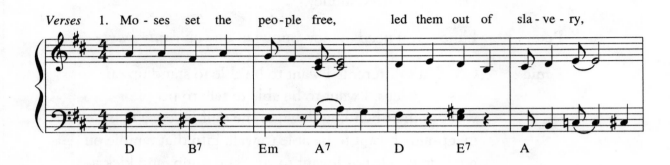

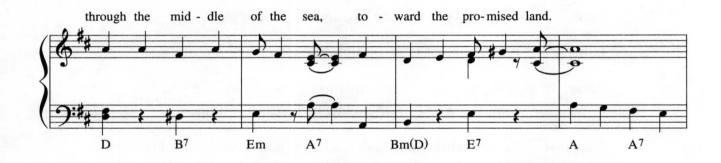

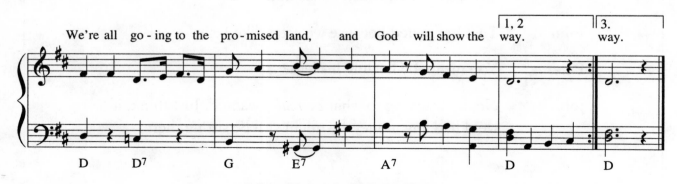

1. Moses set the people free,
   led them out of slavery,
   through the middle of the sea,
   toward the promised land.

   Refrain
   We're all going to the promised land.
   We're all going to the promised land.
   We're all going to the promised land,
   and God will show the way.

2. In the desert's heat and dust,
   people grumbled, moaned and fussed,
   Moses said, 'In God we trust;
   let's find the promised land.'

   Refrain

3. Through the desert they were led
   by the cloud and fire ahead,
   then one day the lookout said,
   'We've found the promised land.'

   Refrain

STAND UP! WALK TALL!

Text: Michael Forster
Music: Christopher Tambling

Refrain

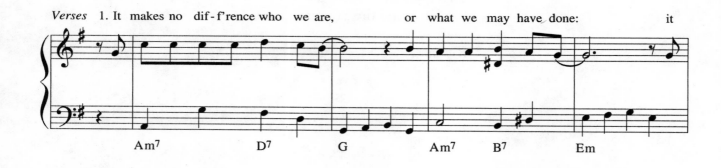

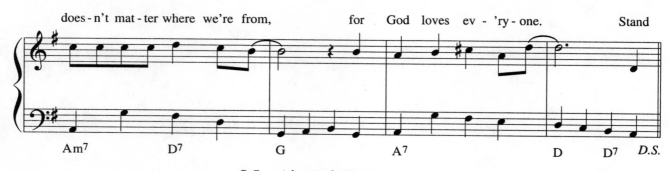

Refrain
Stand up! Walk tall in the house of God!
Stand up! Walk tall in the house of God!
Stand up! Walk tall in the house of God
and say that we belong!

1. It makes no diff'rence who we are,
   or what we may have done:
   it doesn't matter where we're from,
   for God loves everyone.

Refrain

2. Whatever people think or say,
   we need not be afraid.
   We're members of the human race,
   the people God has made.

Refrain

3. So, male or female, black or white,
   of any class or race,
   we're not afraid to stand up straight
   and look God in the face!

Refrain

THERE WASN'T ANY ROOM AT THE INN

Text: Michael Forster
Music: Christopher Tambling

1. Mary said to Joseph,
   'Let's find a place to stay,
    for it's much too cold to sleep outside
   with a baby on the way!'

   Refrain
   There wasn't any room at the inn.
   There wasn't any room at the inn.
   They couldn't find a bed
   for a weary mother's head
   in the whole of Bethlehem!

2. Joseph said to Mary,
   'I hope we'll find a place,
   but the town is full of visitors
   and there's not a lot of space.'

   Refrain

3. Then they found a stable,
   a simple little shed,
   and the Saviour of the world was born
   with a manger for his bed!

   Refrain

WHATEVER YOU'VE DONE, I LOVE YOU

Text: Michael Forster
Music: Christopher Tambling

1. The son said, 'Father, I've been bad,
   and now it's made me very sad;
   I've lost the good things I once had,'
   and his father said, 'I love you.'

   Refrain
   'Whatever you've done, I love you,
   whatever you've done, I love you,
   whatever you've done, I love you,
   that's what love's about.'

2. The son said, 'After what I've done,
   I know I can't be called your son;
   I'll work for you like anyone,'
   and his father said, 'I love you.'

   Refrain

3. They threw a party, very grand,
   with dancing and a proper band!
   The son said, 'I don't understand,'
   and his father said, 'I love you.'

   Refrain

Well, Well, Well!

Text: Michael Forster
To the tune of *Three Blind Mice*

Well, well, well!
Well, well, well!
Jesus sat down,
Jesus sat down,
beside a well in the open air,
and met a Samaritan woman there,
he said, 'Have you got any water to share?'
Oh, well, well, well!

Well, well, well!
Well, well, well!
Here's what she said,
Here's what she said,
'It's not as simple as that, you see,
we live and we worship so diff'rently,
I don't think that you should be talking to me.'
Oh, well, well, well!

Well, well, well!
Well, well, well!
Jesus replied,
Jesus replied,
'If I were you I would talk to me,
because I can offer you life, you see;
your fear is a prison and love is the key.'
Oh, well, well, well!

Well, well, well!
Well, well, well!
Listen to him!
Listen to him!
We all belong to the human race,
whatever our faith or our shade of face!
It's time that we learnt about sharing our space.
Oh, well, well, well!

Ride That Camel! Chase That Star!

Text: Michael Forster
To the tune of *Twinkle, Twinkle Little Star*

Wise men from a country far,
Ride that camel! Chase that star!
Through the lonely desert night
it will be your guiding light.
Wise men from a country far,
Ride that camel! Chase that star!

Wise men from a country far,
Ride that camel! Chase that star!
Incense, gold and myrrh you bring,
presents for the baby king.
Wise men from a country far,
Ride that camel! Chase that star!

Wise men from a country far,
Ride that camel! Chase that star!
Follow where it goes before,
on the desert myst'ry tour!
Wise men from a country far,
Ride that camel! Chase that star!

Sing a Song of Weather!

Text: Michael Forster
To the tune of *Sing a Song of Sixpence*

Sing a song of weather,
of wind and snow and rain;
lovely summer sunshine,
(now and again!)
Changes in the weather can catch us on the hop;
what a pity we can't tell the wind and rain to stop!

Sing a song of weather,
for even rain and snow
keep the garden healthy,
help make things grow:
food for us to eat, and grass where we can play;
what a good thing we can't tell the rain to go away!

Thank You, O God, For All Our Friends

Text: Michael Forster
To the tune of *Here we go Round the Mulberry Bush*

(Before you sing, what kind of morning is it?)

Thank you, O God, for all our friends,
for all our friends,
for all our friends,
thank you, O God, for all our friends,
on a *cold and frosty**
warm and sunny
dark and murky
damp and rainy
foggy, misty
morning!

Thank you, O God, for flow'rs and trees

Thank you, O God, for animals

*Use whichever is appropriate